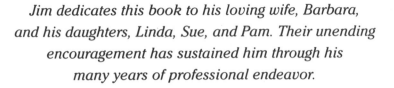

*Jim dedicates this book to his loving wife, Barbara,
and his daughters, Linda, Sue, and Pam. Their unending
encouragement has sustained him through his
many years of professional endeavor.*

*Judith dedicates this book to her husband, Joe; to their children,
Jennifer, Patrick, Cathy Jean, Chris, Cari, and Cori; to extended
family; and to friends and colleagues who have inspired her
work and recommitted it to the education of everyone's children.*

*Tony dedicates this book to Sandra, Elizabeth, and Nicholas,
who remind him every day of what is important.*

A Performance-Based Approach
to Teacher Development and
School Improvement

Supervision for LEARNING

James M. Aseltine
Judith O. Faryniarz
Anthony J. Rigazio-DiGilio

Association for Supervision and Curriculum Development
Alexandria, Virginia USA

Association for Supervision and Curriculum Development
1703 N. Beauregard St. • Alexandria, VA 22311-1714 USA
Phone: 800-933-2723 or 703-578-9600 • Fax: 703-575-5400
Web site: www.ascd.org • E-mail: member@ascd.org
Author guidelines: www.ascd.org/write

Gene R. Carter, *Executive Director;* Nancy Modrak, *Director of Publishing;* Julie Houtz, *Director of Book Editing & Production;* Katie Martin, *Project Manager;* Shelley Kirby, *Senior Graphic Designer;* Barton Matheson Willse & Worthington, *Typesetter;* Vivian Coss, *Production Specialist*

All Web links in this book are correct as of the publication date below but may have become inactive or otherwise modified since that time. If you notice a deactivated or changed link, please e-mail books@ascd.org with the words "Link Update" in the subject line. In your message, please specify the Web link, the book title, and the page number on which the link appears.

ASCD Member Book, No. FY06-7 (May 2006, P). ASCD Member Books mail to Premium (P), Comprehensive (C), and Regular (R) members on this schedule: Jan., PC; Feb., P; Apr., PCR; May, P; July, PC; Aug., P; Sept., PCR; Nov., PC; Dec., P.

PAPERBACK ISBN-13: 978-1-4166-0327-6   ASCD product #106001
PAPERBACK ISBN-10: 1-4166-0327-1
Also available as an e-book through ebrary, netLibrary, and many online booksellers (see Books in Print for the ISBNs).

Quantity discounts for the paperback edition only: 10–49 copies, 10%; 50+ copies, 15%; for 1,000 or more copies, call 800-933-2723, ext. 5634, or 703-575-5634. For desk copies: member@ascd.org.

Library of Congress Cataloging-in-Publication Data

Aseltine, James M.
   Supervision for learning : a performance-based approach to teacher development and school improvement / James M. Aseltine, Judith O. Faryniarz, and Anthony J. Rigazio-DiGilio.
      p. cm.
   Includes bibliographical references and index.
   ISBN-13: 978-1-4166-0327-6 (pbk. : alk. paper)
   ISBN-10: 1-4166-0327-1 (pbk. : alk. paper)   1. Teachers—Rating of—United States.
2. Teachers—In-service training—United States.   I. Faryniarz, Judith O., 1951–
II. Rigazio-DiGilio, Anthony J., 1952–   III. Title.

   LB2838.A765 2006
   371.2′03–dc22

                                                                                2006003153

15 14 13 12 11 10 09 08 07 06   1 2 3 4 5 6 7 8 9 10 11 12

Supervision for LEARNING

Foreword

I clearly recall the ritual from my early experiences as a teacher. Twice a year, my principal would visit my classroom, sit in the back, and observe me at work for 20-odd minutes. While trying to appear "natural" and concentrate on my lesson, I could not help but notice him scrutinizing the room and making notations on his clipboard. A day or two later, I would receive a filled-in copy of the district's Teacher Observation Form with some perfunctory comments ("Has good rapport with students") and a SATISFACTORY rating stamped at the bottom of the page in purple ink.

Don't get me wrong: I liked my principal and he liked me. I never felt that the observation and evaluation process was adversarial; I just did not perceive these biannual "snapshots" to be a particularly worthwhile experience for either of us. The unspoken truth was that virtually all teachers in my school were certified as SATISFACTORY, provided that they weren't the target of too many parental complaints and that they could be counted on to address the majority of behavior problems in the classroom instead of bumping them to the front office.

For me, the most influential professional growth experiences occurred informally, as I picked the brain of an effective veteran teacher or when I had the opportunity to work with a colleague to co-plan an activity or a performance. In stark contrast, my "official" professional development experiences consisted primarily of large-scale events. My fellow staff members and I were herded into the high school auditorium, where we spent the morning listening to a motivating speaker before breaking into afternoon workshops, the content of which was primarily determined by what volunteer leaders wished to offer. I fondly recall one very popular offering: a "Color Me Beautiful" seminar sponsored by an enterprising teacher who moonlighted as a wardrobe consultant!

Fast forward 30-some years. Educators today are immersed in a decidedly different world. The emergence of content and performance standards, coupled with high-stakes accountability systems, has shifted the professional focus from "inputs" and "process" to "results." These not-so-subtle shifts affect nearly all facets of our work, including professional development, teacher evaluation, and approaches to improve school effectiveness.

It is the current state of educational affairs that makes *Supervision for Learning* such a timely and significant work. The authors marry the analytic insight of scholars with the practical wisdom of veteran educators as they first make the case for shifting to a "performance-based" model of supervision and evaluation and then show how it's done. *Supervision for Learning* offers a refreshing alternative to the ritualistic and marginally effective evaluation practices that teachers and administrators have endured for years. And significantly, the book proposes a pathway toward true *professional* development: one that honors the professionalism of teachers while concurrently targeting the achievement needs of learners. Its focus on student achievement looks beyond the narrow tunnel of standardized test scores and toward a broader view of "data" inclusive of authentic student work and genuine accomplishments on the part of teacher and student.

Although their tone is optimistic, the authors do not shy away from the less than rosy realities faced by leaders in most schools. They tackle such challenges as resistant staff members and deficient teachers and offer concrete guidance, tools, and practical strategies to help everyone reap the benefits of this approach.

This book deserves "must read" attention from school leaders at all levels who value the continuous learning of their staff and pursue continuous learning themselves. Follow the precepts and practices contained within these pages, and you will realize a more effective use of your supervisory energies while guiding *true* professional development in the service of student learning.

Jay McTighe

Acknowledgments

The development of Performance-Based Supervision and Evaluation, past and present, relies on the contributions of far more educators and friends than those most immediately involved in writing this book. We wish to thank the leaders of the national and state professional organizations who have set the parameters of the current discussion; the theorists and practitioner-scholars who have described propitious routes toward success; the key personnel at the Connecticut State Department of Education who have provided the conceptual tools to chart new directions; and the many teachers and administrators in districts throughout the United States who were willing to set aside conventional ways, take risks, and work hard to improve instruction and enhance student learning. Our model continues to develop because of the efforts of professionals at all levels of the educational enterprise to align our work with student learning. Thank you for your dedication to promoting learning for all students and participating in the reculturation of our profession.

Sincere thanks are also in order to those who have helped with this book's development. In particular, we are grateful to our friends at ASCD: Sally Chapman, for her encouragement and counsel; Scott Willis, for his support and suggestions as the manuscript came together; and Katie Martin, for her tireless efforts to sharpen each section of the book and present a cohesive message for our readers. We purposefully submitted our manuscript proposal to ASCD because of the organization's commitment to the professional development of its membership. We continue to be impressed by and grateful for this.

Finally, we extend our heartfelt gratitude to our spouses, families, and friends for their support and encouragement during the many months needed to complete this manuscript. You have patiently supported long hours at the computer and in authors' meetings because you believed in us and the importance of our work. You have our deep and enduring love and gratitude.

Introduction

As teachers and administrators, we came to understand the process of supervision and evaluation through a fairly common set of experiences. As teachers, we met with our supervisor at the beginning of each academic year to determine a mutually agreeable focus for professional growth. As the year progressed, we dutifully kept the administration up to date with our progress, and we incorporated their suggestions into our efforts. Usually, our supervisor observed us teaching during the year and provided written feedback, although the lessons observed may have had little to do with our professional development plan. And, of course, there was the end-of-the-year "write up": the summative evaluation required for our personnel files.

Over the past 10 years, the world of education has changed dramatically. In this era of mandated standardized testing and federal legislation, such as the No Child Left Behind Act of 2001, there has never been greater accountability for the work that teachers and administrators do. Here in the United States, curricula across the country reflect the impact of the content and performance standards developed by professional organizations, states, and local school districts. More than ever, there is a focus on comparing student performance to accepted standards, paying close attention to test data, and forming strategic plans to improve student performance. Furthermore, our students' parents and our communities are more focused than ever on what is happening in our classrooms and whether our students are being adequately prepared for higher education and life beyond school. As educators, we must be able to say with certainty that our students are

- Learning challenging content at high levels of understanding;
- Developing essential skills and competencies, particularly in communication;
- Evolving in their capacity to think critically, solve problems creatively, and integrate new learning into prior knowledge; and
- Developing strong interpersonal and intrapersonal skills that support their connections to family, community, and the world of work.

With this new paradigm in mind, we have developed an approach to supervision and evaluation that helps build educators' capacity to address student learning needs. It underscores the professionalism of teaching by asking teachers to take a more active role in determining the focus of their professional efforts, and it places student learning at the heart of this focus.

To explain the historical context for our model, we offer a playful analogy. Consider: *How is teacher evaluation like the game of golf?*

When we ask this question of teachers and administrators, they generally offer two different types of responses. Teachers tend to respond that, like golf, both the history and the process of teacher evaluation are pretty boring. We have heard teachers joke that the evaluation process can leave them feeling like they're "in the rough" or like they're the golf ball itself: whacked around only to end up in the hole. Others observe that teacher evaluation, like each round of play, is very imprecise, yet the routines of play seldom change. Administrators tend to note that golf and teacher evaluation both require forethought, knowledge, and skill. But unlike golf, teacher evaluation rarely has a 19th hole; when one round is complete, everything starts anew.

Humor aside, it *is* possible to trace the history of teacher evaluation using analogies to the game of golf. For the better part of the past century—through the 1960s—teacher evaluation was similar to "putting around": relatively casual and without firm rules. Districts typically used a system that enabled administrators to record their observations of many characteristics of "good" classrooms: things like all student desks in straight rows, legible teacher penmanship, and artfully designed bulletin boards. Although some districts looked carefully at the qualities of teaching and learning, the majority of supervisors' efforts were guided by their knowledge of instruction—or, as it ended up being communicated to teachers, by their personal knowledge of classroom management. This resulted in supervisory feedback that was focused more on the qualities of the classroom environment than on improving teaching and learning. Some administrators observed all teachers over the course of several full lessons; others handed teachers blank observation forms at the close of the school year, asked for signatures, and promised that the forms would be completed over the summer. Generally speaking, this type of "putting around" did not move educational practice to a higher level.

In 1969, concerned by the lack of professionalism associated with the common practices of teacher evaluation, a group of Harvard researchers headed by Robert Goldhammer formulated a more systematic approach to teacher evaluation. Called "clinical supervision," this model advocated involving the teacher in setting goals and determining assessment methods (Wiles & Bondi, 2002). Not long after, the Goldhammer model of clinical supervision was eclipsed by one devised by Madeline Hunter. While Goldhammer's process emphasized the teacher's role in selecting areas of focus and evaluation criteria, Hunter's presented external criteria, purportedly based on empirical research in educational psychology, and emphasized the supervisor's role as objective observer (Nolan & Hoover, 2004).

The tenor of the educational times contributed to the broader acceptance of Hunter's work. By the mid-1970s, the "Back to Basics" trend was sweeping the United States, and many districts and states adopted the process–product formulation of the Hunter model. States like North Carolina, California, Texas, and Connecticut led the way with low-inference observation instruments that could be used in any classroom situation. These models required administrators to take full notes on the lesson; analyze those notes using the prescribed categories of effective teaching; and finally, rate the teacher's performance and share this information in a post-observation conference. Quite the opposite of the "putting around" of previous decades, these systems of teacher supervision and evaluation provided focused, detailed, and meaningful data about the quality of teaching.

For beginning teachers and those experiencing difficulties in the classroom, the clarity that these low-inference clinical supervision models provide was—and frankly remains—very helpful. Because clinical supervision models can reveal deficiencies in teachers' skill sets, they are an effective way to promote mastery of the basic elements of teaching and classroom management. In terms of our golf analogy, they are like "drivers"—the powerful clubs that allow a golfer to cover a lot of territory on the fairway and advance significantly toward the green. However, although clinical supervision models do seem to have some positive effect on student growth, they have not achieved the levels their proponents touted they would. They also have inherent limitations, such as the dynamic between formative supervision and summative evaluation, and the challenge of acquiring the resources necessary for a full program of supervision (Oliva & Pawlas, 2004).

Every golfer knows that it takes more than a putter and a set of drivers to successfully traverse a golf course. What is needed is a set of "irons"—the versatile tools that allow one to play the short game, to set up the green shots so that putting can be more efficient. In education, our "short game" is a more refined approach to professional growth and a clear focus on student learning. After all, Peterson (2000) projects that as many as 94 percent of classroom teachers are already technically capable in their instructional skills. For these teachers, the traditional forms of teacher evaluation (putters and drivers) are less than professionally meaningful, seldom produce student growth, and rarely contribute to the teaching and learning capacity of the school.

Happily, the last several years have seen the further development of supervision and evaluation models that offer procedural options for both teachers and supervisors. These methods, such as action research, peer coaching, walk-throughs, and lesson study, can be tailored to the teacher's specific developmental level and curriculum area, providing a great variety of options to meet the unique needs of individuals within the context of the school environment. Like a set of irons in golf, they offer a range of precision that can focus the teacher's attention on refining the qualitative aspects of teaching and learning—aspects often overlooked within traditional forms of teacher assessment. This book is about how to use the irons, how to play the personal game of professional growth, and how to remain focused on the goal of improved student learning. It's about helping technically competent instructors to become master teachers. It focuses supervision on student learning by using classroom data to promote teacher learning.

With that in mind, our approach is grounded in a number of carefully considered assumptions:

• Children learn best when new learning is connected to prior knowledge, instruction builds on that knowledge and addresses learning needs, and assessment informs instruction.

• Effective teaching and assessment reflect challenging expectations for learning, are connected to rigorous content and performance standards, and are at the center of school improvement efforts.

• Change occurs from the inside out, meaning that professional growth takes time, cannot be rushed, and demands personal energy and reflective practice.

• Changes in teacher behavior lead to changes in teacher attitudes (DuFour & Eaker, 1998).

• What teachers learn by working on a strategically chosen "slice" of student learning can be generalized to their broader teaching responsibilities.

The new model we offer is called Performance-Based Supervision and Evaluation (PBSE). We genuinely believe that the techniques associated with this model can help "reprofessionalize" the work of teachers and provide efficient strategies to increase the analytic and instructional capacity of schools and school districts. The model was developed and first implemented in our home state of Connecticut, where it proved an effective means of strengthening teaching and student learning, and enhancing professional culture. To illustrate how PBSE can be used as supervision for learning, three full case studies of the model's implementation are available on the ASCD Web site: www.ascd.org. These studies focus on the sustained implementation of PBSE in varying environments: a suburban middle school, an urban school district, and a statewide vocational-technical school system. Across all three environments, the results were the same:

• Student achievement consistently improved, as evidenced by performance on local assessments and state standardized tests.

• Teacher capacity for making strategic instructional interventions based on student performance data increased.

• Teacher professional development became far more connected to student learning needs.

• Teachers and administrators become more focused and self-directed, which changed both their supervisory conversations and the way in which they completed their professional responsibilities.

• Student achievement, teacher development, and administrator development became closely linked to school improvement practices.

In this book, we offer a roadmap for both teachers and administrators as they embark upon the challenge of this model of supervision and evaluation. Throughout, we draw your attention to the "keystones" of our model: the foundational components that set it apart from other approaches to supervision and evaluation. Finally, we offer extended looks at Performance-Based Supervision and Evaluation in action by sharing the stories of one school's first year of PBSE implementation. The educators we describe are composites, but their experiences are representative of the teachers and principals with whom we have worked.

A shift to a performance-based approach to supervision and evaluation demands the commitment and energy of both teachers and supervisors. As you will see in the chapters ahead, what makes this new paradigm worth the effort is that it integrates many aspects of current best practice into a comprehensive initiative to improve student learning: focusing on essential understandings, using student data to make instructional decisions, encouraging teacher leadership through action research, developing a culture of collaboration to improve student achievement, and promoting reflective practice. It is not another initiative to add to the improvement plans a school is already undertaking; instead, it is an effective way to achieve the goals themselves.

1

Reconceptualizing Supervision and Evaluation

◢ Marcia Williams, an 8th grade social studies teacher at Fairview Middle School, organized her students' papers into a neat bundle, ready for grading. Her "Period C" class had just left the room, and she could now turn her thoughts to the meeting she had scheduled for her planning period. It was mid-September and time to meet with Fairview's principal, Gary Mulholland, to discuss her professional objectives for the school year ahead.

At Marcia's end-of-year meeting with her principal last spring, Gary had shared his excitement about a different way of approaching the whole process of supervision and evaluation. Just a month earlier, he and his colleague administrators had taken part in a professional development program that provided in-depth information and simulation activities in a process called Performance-Based Supervision and Evaluation (PBSE). The gist of it, Gary had explained, was collaborative effort between a teacher and supervisor to align the teacher's annual development plan with explicit student learning needs: choosing an area of "essential learning," analyzing related performance data, identifying a specific learning need within that area, and pursuing the professional development necessary to address that need more effectively. He had become convinced that this process would improve student performance at Fairview and dramatically enhance the teachers' capacity for effective instruction and assessment. Gary had arranged for his teachers to have their own training in the process during the two professional development days in August.

Her principal's enthusiasm had been contagious, and Marcia had approached the August professional development session with an open mind and a curious spirit. After the workshop, she had found Performance-Based

Supervision and Evaluation even more appealing. To Marcia, the model made sense, connected with many of the best-practice recommendations she continued to hear and read about, and seemed realistic about the challenges of the classroom. Most of all, she liked the model's consistent focus on student learning and building teacher capacity to address student learning needs.

But as much as the PBSE model appealed to her, Marcia was unsure about how to begin using it herself. She had thought about the model as she considered potential areas for professional growth, but the annual plan she was about to propose to her principal was more a reflection of her old habits than the new approach. She had decided to focus on furthering her students' understanding of economic globalization. In light of current events, this certainly seemed to be an authentic and appropriate consideration for social studies. It was part of the 8th grade curriculum and a topic that she found personally interesting. In addition, Marcia's 8th grade team was a close-knit group, and her colleagues had expressed interest in working on a year-long theme—perhaps one related to world issues. Economic globalization seemed to fit the bill.

Marcia arrived at her meeting with the principal with a proposed professional objective in hand. She began to explain a number of possible professional development activities, including reading about the world economy, collecting related newspaper and magazine articles and sharing them with students, investigating guest speakers who might present "real life" information about domestic and worldwide economic changes, and holding weekly team meetings to discuss how the global economy theme might be addressed in math, science, and language arts classes. She noted that she would assess her students' deepening understanding of economic globalization by engaging them in discussion around the topic at least once per marking period and taking notes on what they had to say. And as evidence of her professional growth, she would collect artifacts of her instructional efforts, including students' assessments and comments, and share them with the principal once at mid-year and again at the end of the year.

When Marcia had finished explaining her idea, Gary smiled and took a breath. Marcia's plan was timely, authentic, collaborative, and focused on enriching the 8th grade curriculum. It was fully in line with the type of supervisory process he had used with staff members for many years. But it was not in line with the plan to implement Performance-Based Supervision and Evaluation. To bring Marcia on board, he would need to help her bridge the divide between past practices and the new approach: one grounded in analysis of student performance data, results-driven change, and a commitment to building instructional and organizational capacity. ◪

The State of Supervision and Evaluation

Teacher supervision and evaluation is an important focus for principals and other administrators. Since the 1960s, our body of professional knowledge on this topic has grown, supported by the work of Acheson and Gall (1997), Goldhammer, Anderson, and Krawjewski (1993), McGreal (1983), Manatt and Manatt (1984), Peterson (2000), Stanley and Popham (1998), Hunter (1976), Eisner (2002), Scriven (1981), Stufflebeam (1991), and other pioneers. We have come to understand more clearly the nature and importance of specific aspects of quality teaching, such as building on prior learning, effective questioning techniques, productive and intellectually challenging activities, and reinforcement of lesson objectives (Marzano, 2003). We can identify student engagement, self- and peer assessment, and the opportunity for children to work collaboratively as important components of effective classrooms. Most classroom teachers believe that both children and adults need to take an active role in their own learning. And our professional vocabulary has embraced terms such as "constructivist learning," "discovery learning," "cooperative learning," "differentiated instruction," and "multiple intelligences."

Given the historical focus on instructional processes, it is understandable that many current supervisory practices look primarily at curriculum and instruction: what the students are learning and how they are learning it. This focus is evident in the typical pattern of supervision and evaluation: a new goal at the start of the school year; periodic classroom observation, with formal and informal feedback; mid-year and end-of-year meetings to discuss progress toward the goal; and the supervisor's end-of-year evaluation report that comments on the teacher's accomplishments and perhaps lays the groundwork for next year's focus.

This traditional process is not without merit. One-on-one goal discussions with a supervisor help teachers understand what school leaders believe to be important for professional growth.

The traditional process also provides performance feedback and underscores that teachers are accountable for the work they do with students. In addition, the process acknowledges teachers' professionalism by giving them some latitude in choosing what they want to work on for the year and asking them to develop learning experiences related to that professional focus.

The Call for an Alternative Model

So why revisit supervisory practices? Why do we need a different paradigm for teacher evaluation? Here are some reasons to consider.

1. *The focus in education has shifted from the centrality of teaching to the importance of student learning.* Over the past 10 years, this idea has been embraced not only by educators, but also by parents, communities, and legislators. The now-widespread use of content standards as benchmarks for student learning is a prime indicator. National professional organizations, state departments of education, and many local school districts have identified and publicized what students should know and be able to do at each grade and within grade clusters for many of the content areas.

2. *We live in an age of ever-greater accountability.* There is near-ubiquitous sentiment that educators need to demonstrate through performance that their efforts are resulting in student learning. Educators are expected to be able to prove that students are learning what they need to know at challenging levels of understanding and as a result of what and how teachers are teaching.

3. *Education literature and professional development initiatives are increasingly focused on data-based decision making.* For the classroom teacher, data-based decision making means looking at student work carefully and analytically and using the findings to inform instructional planning. Yet, many teachers have not received the training they need to confidently examine student work from an analytical perspective.

4. *Traditional models of supervision and evaluation focus on the process of teachers' work rather than its outcome.* During traditional

classroom observations, supervisors are the persons collecting data: they take notes, analyze those notes, give feedback and direction, and write up a report. Outside of any pre- and post-observation conferencing, teachers rarely participate in analyzing and drawing conclusions from these data or, more importantly, from student performance data.

5. *The traditional emphasis on instructional processes delimits teachers' professional growth.* Once classroom teachers become familiar with and even expert in effective teaching strategies, they usually maintain their proficiency but are less likely to continue refining their practices and striving for further improvement. It's certainly true that many master teachers use their considerable instructional skills to great effect in their classrooms, and perhaps even mentor colleagues new to the profession, but their own professional growth curve often flattens. Then there are the cases of teachers whose knowledge of classroom pedagogy has surpassed that of their supervisors' and who must determine future professional challenges on their own.

6. *Traditional teacher supervision and evaluation may not explicitly link instruction and student learning or provide for differentiated instructional contexts.* As in our opening scenario, teachers' intentions are typically laudable when it comes to selecting a worthy focus for professional growth. However, to make a real difference in student learning, supervisors and teachers must follow a more strategic and contextualized process. Even when a teacher's plan involves collecting verbal student feedback, the relative lack of performance data makes it difficult to gauge how much of an impact those efforts really have on student learning. In addition, a more traditional protocol for supervision and evaluation is basically a "one size fits all" approach; the supervisor's similar pattern of involvement and interaction with all members of the teaching staff—meet, observe, comment, evaluate—limits the opportunities to help each teacher achieve maximum growth.

7. *Traditional methods of teacher evaluation rarely help teachers make a direct link between their professional growth and what the*

standardized test results and school improvement plan indicate are the real student learning needs. A teacher's draft goal may be appropriate for her curriculum area, but is it appropriate for her particular group of students and their learning needs? Will it benefit them when they encounter standards-based assessments? Will it help the school achieve its overall improvement goals? Linking the work of many faculty members through the focused goals of the school improvement plan helps create a sense of professional community in which members from diverse curriculum areas can contribute to the growth of all students. When all teachers are working on meaningful and connected goals—goals that are measurable and directly linked to the overall mission of the school—then real progress will be possible for all students, not just those fortunate enough to be in a specific teacher's classroom.

An Overview of Performance-Based Supervision and Evaluation

The process of supervision for learning described in this book offers both teachers and their supervisors the opportunity to work together to improve student learning. It draws on assessment research (Darling-Hammond, 1996; Iwanicki, 1998; Peterson, 2000; Stiggins, 1989) and extends best practices in teacher supervision and evaluation in the following ways:

- It focuses more on instructional *results* than instructional *processes.*
- It emphasizes setting meaningful and achievable professional goals, measured in terms of improved student performance.
- It asks educators to individually and collectively analyze student work, and use these data to address learning needs in areas of essential knowledge and skill throughout the curriculum.
- It asks teachers to design focused interventions to strengthen and enhance student learning in the target area.

• It asks teachers to develop a plan for continuing professional growth that is related to the focus for improved student performance and that further establishes them as role models of lifelong learning.

• It requires teachers to use evidence of student performance to demonstrate that learning has taken place.

• It marshals the power of mutual collaboration and commitment by the teacher, the supervisor, and additional "expert resources."

• It links the work of classroom teachers with the goals of the school improvement plan.

——————————— ▽ KEYSTONE ———————————

Performance-Based Supervision and Evaluation requires teachers to reconsider their approach to their work. It asks them to make different decisions and use different procedures; to focus narrowly and deeply on content related to essential learning; and to commit to improving their diagnostic and problem-solving skills along with their instructional skills.

An Introduction to the Criteria of Excellence

Fundamental to Performance-Based Supervision and Evaluation are the "Criteria of Excellence." These Criteria, found in their entirety in Appendix A, identify key processes, competencies, and achievements that the teacher and supervisor will accomplish through their work together. They are organized into six phases, or distinct components, of a full cycle of teacher growth.

Teacher Preparation. This is the process by which the teacher begins to collect information about student learning needs and to develop an emerging idea for a clear, narrow, and standards-based area of essential learning as an appropriate focus for an improvement objective.

Initial Collaboration. The teacher and supervisor analyze student data more deeply and finalize the focus and details of the improvement objective and the professional development plan.

Initial Monitoring. The teacher begins to participate in professional development and to implement strategies that support student learning, making necessary adjustments as the process unfolds.

Mid-Cycle Review. At mid-year, or another appropriate midpoint, the teacher and supervisor review progress to date, examining artifacts related to teacher initiatives and, if possible, student work, and modifying the plan as needed.

Secondary Monitoring. The teacher continues to carry out the professional development plan and deepens learning related to student needs by using more refined assessment methods to inform instructional decisions.

Summative Review. At the end of each cycle, the teacher and supervisor review evidence linking teaching strategies to student learning outcomes, and develop written reflections that detail teacher growth and suggest ideas for further development in the next cycle.

At first glance, the Criteria of Excellence resemble a traditional cycle of teacher supervision and evaluation: a professional development objective is established and the teacher and supervisor meet at a midpoint and end point to review the teacher's progress. That said, they are distinguished by two important purposes:

1. The Criteria of Excellence establish a clear process for supervision and evaluation, offering a generally sequential roadmap for the teacher and supervisor to follow throughout their work together. Significantly, this process mirrors the full cycle of what may be termed "applied action research," with the overarching intent to bring about improved teaching practice as evidenced by improved student performance.

2. The Criteria of Excellence make explicit the knowledge and skills associated with teacher development to improve student

learning, establishing a set of standards that can be used to assess and track a teacher's growing expertise. Each phase of the Criteria outlines several associated competencies or accomplishments (called indicators); supervisors and teachers may judge a teacher's competency with each indicator as "competent," "emerging," or "just beginning." Underlying this purpose of the Criteria is the assumption that an effective teacher is one who judiciously and systematically uses pupil performance data to inform modifications and improvements in practice.

The chapters that follow offer a more detailed portrait of how the Criteria of Excellence work in practice, with special emphasis on the Teacher Preparation, Initial Collaboration, and Summative Review Phases. The Initial Monitoring Phase, Mid-Cycle Review Phase, and Secondary Monitoring Phase, while less fully detailed in this text, contribute to the cycle of professional growth by providing an opportunity for the teacher to acquire and apply new learning, collect and analyze student performance data, and receive formative feedback from the supervisor and perhaps other resource personnel as well.

Because each teacher's professional maturity is unique, the Criteria necessarily offer some flexibility. They are a clear guide for the work of the teacher and supervisor, but they are not prescriptive. While working within any phase of the Criteria, the teacher and supervisor may decide that the teacher needs additional professional learning to achieve full competence for any specific indicator. However, it may not be necessary for the teacher to be fully competent with every indicator in sequence before she participates in other activities outlined in the Criteria of Excellence. For example, although a teacher may be working on the preliminary skills of identifying essential areas of learning and analyzing student performance data (associated with indicators in the Teacher Preparation Phase), she will still create a plan for professional development (associated with indicators in the Initial Collaboration Phase) and go on to review new learning and accomplishments with her supervisor at mid-cycle and end-of-cycle conferences (associated, respectively, with indicators in the Mid-Cycle and Summative Review Phases).

KEYSTONE

Performance-Based Supervision and Evaluation gives teachers a higher degree of control over the evaluation process as they work on a self-selected improvement objective aimed at bringing their students to higher levels of knowledge and understanding. In doing so, they determine not only what teaching and learning data will be the focus of their professional reflections, but also the agenda for supervisory discussions. Over time, this capacity for using student data analytically to improve teaching and learning empowers the whole of the teachers' work.

The "Supervisor" in Performance-Based Supervision and Evaluation

In the chapters ahead, we follow the story of Marcia Williams and two of her colleagues at Fairview Middle School as they use the PBSE process to enhance their own instructional capacity for improving student learning. As you will see, all three educators work most directly with their primary supervisor, the building principal. We realize that in various districts, different types of administrators serve as "primary" or "contributing" (secondary) supervisors in their work with faculty, and we use the broad term "supervisor" throughout the book.

Typically, a building-level administrator, such as the principal, assistant principal, "house" principal, and the like, will serve as a teacher's primary supervisor within the process. Proximity suggests that this administrator will be in a strong position to communicate easily with the teacher, observe her work firsthand, and offer appropriate guidance. However, an administrator who is more of a "generalist" educator may not have the specific content knowledge to effectively coach all faculty members, particularly those working in music, art, special education, school psychology, and other specialized areas of professional responsibility. In these cases, a district administrator with expertise in the targeted content area may well serve as the primary supervisor. When this is the case, collaboration between the off-site primary supervisor and the building-level contributing administrator is a crucial factor in supporting the teacher's growth in content knowledge and general pedagogy, and in arriving at a balanced judgment of the teacher's work.

Performance-Based Supervision and Evaluation and the Local District's Plan

All districts have an articulated plan for how teachers and other district personnel will be supervised and evaluated. Some districts implement these plans to the letter; others treat them more as loose guidelines. Performance-Based Supervision and Evaluation offers an instructive process that can be integrated into a district's present system:

• When teachers and supervisors focus their PBSE work on improving teaching and learning, classroom observations are purposeful and related to the teacher's professional development plan. They become an opportunity for the supervisor to collect related data, to observe for specific elements of effective teaching, and to offer focused feedback.

• The model supports collaboration and collegial discourse about student learning and is directly linked to the school improvement process.

• PBSE is appropriate for use with teachers and administrators at all stages of their careers; specific growth targets and interventions can be differentiated according to individual learning, group, or team needs.

Make no mistake about it: this is challenging work. For this process of supervision and evaluation to be successful, both teachers and administrators need to study the process, work through the phases, and support each other in the effort to improve student learning. This demands mutual commitment, energy, and trust, as well as a willingness to be accountable for the results of one's efforts. Nonetheless, the potential rewards are great: demonstrated professional competence and growth that result in improved student learning and greater organizational capacity for change. Our students deserve nothing less.

2

Getting Ready to
Target Improvement

This chapter focuses on getting started with Performance-Based Supervision and Evaluation. The first steps in the process involve the teacher's efforts to examine student performance on standardized assessments and classroom assignments and then determine a focus for her professional work throughout the year.

Where to Begin? With the Students!

Traditional models of teacher supervision and evaluation focus on the teacher and on teaching. They begin with an examination of the teacher's current proficiencies and next look at which aspects of effective teaching need continuing support and which need further attention and improvement. Some annual professional development plans are designed around an area of new learning that is personally interesting to the teacher or that reflects an instructional method newly popularized by professional organizations or consultants. Although these approaches are not without merit, they do not necessarily connect with the needs of the teacher's current students.

Performance-Based Supervision and Evaluation *begins* with those students' needs. To prepare for drafting a professional development plan to share with the supervisor, the teacher first considers the "essential" aspects of the curriculum: what is most important for students to know and be able to do at this particular point in their educational development. In our view, well-crafted content and performance standards developed by national professional organizations and state departments of education provide an important foundation for challenging learning experiences, more advanced skills, and deeper understanding—the outcomes increasingly advocated by educational leaders such as Wiggins and McTighe (1998) and Erickson (2001). Standards are also an important frame of reference for determining areas of essential teaching and learning because they often form the basis for the state testing program.

With the PBSE model, once a teacher has identified an area of essential learning, she targets a specific area of that learning that will become her critical focus, or "improvement objective." In other words, rather than embracing a broad pedagogical initiative fleshed out by a scattershot implementation plan and loosely connected evidence of attainment, the teacher focuses on developing the skills, tools, and knowledge necessary to raise achievement in a specific slice of student learning—a narrow aspect of performance that assessment evidence supports as an area of need and that is also directly linked to standards and in line with district priorities. The ultimate outcome for this focus, or "slice," is a demonstrated performance improvement brought about by the professional development and teaching and learning activities that the teacher and supervisor will plan and carry out.

▽ KEYSTONE

Focusing on a "slice" of teaching and learning supports the teacher's developing pedagogical capacity for analyzing student performance data in general; for designing professional development connected to student learning needs; and for developing instructional interventions that align essential curriculum, related instructional methodology, and the monitoring of student progress. In essence, the PBSE process "operationalizes" content standards. A school or district that undertakes this kind of approach increases teacher capacity and enriches institutional culture.

Finding a Focus

For every teacher, there will likely be a number of areas of student learning that seem to qualify as essential knowledge and skills in need of improvement. The process of choosing a single focus is a matter of increasing personal capacity to analyze student performance data and then identify areas of need explicitly linked to standards and consistent with both school improvement goals and district priorities. As teachers become more knowledgeable about and comfortable with the PBSE approach, they will find themselves able to be increasingly strategic in selecting a focus from among the various learning needs that their students may have.

Four tests, consistent with the work of Wiggins and McTighe (1998), offer a framework for the selection process and ensure that the chosen focus is one that will truly affect student learning. Although we number them for ease of reference, they are distinct and not necessarily sequential ways of thinking about data, designed to help educators make decisions in complex contexts:

• *Test #1: Essential Teaching and Learning.* Does the target represent an area of essential teaching and learning for the teacher's grade level and content area?

• *Test #2: Schoolwide and District Data.* Does an analysis of schoolwide or district performance data suggest that the target is an area needing improvement?

• *Test #3: Classroom Assessments.* Does an analysis of classroom assessment data confirm the target as an area needing improvement?

• *Test #4: The School and District Improvement Plan.* Does the target correspond to an area of emphasis in the district or school's improvement plan?

To explain the four tests fully, we will take a closer look at each, with illustration provided by Fairview Middle School's Marcia Williams.

◢ In September, Marcia and her 8th grade teammates, together with the rest of the faculty, participated in a series of after-school professional development sessions on Performance-Based Supervision and Evaluation as a follow-up to their August inservice training. By the end of these sessions, Marcia was seriously reconsidering the idea of a professional development initiative focused on the global economy. She still thought it was a *worthy* focus, but she also realized that student performance data might argue for something different.

In the weeks since school had started, a new area of need had come to Marcia's attention: writing skills. While discussing the anticipated results of the recently completed round of state standardized testing, several 7th grade teachers commented that the new crop of 8th graders had probably scored very low on the writing sample portion of the test. This group had struggled with writing as 7th graders, their former teachers explained. What's more, they said, these students had unusually low scores on the state writing tests they had taken in 4th grade . . . and had performed only marginally better on the one they'd taken in 6th grade.

This conversation about deficient writing struck a chord with Marcia. It was true that the few short, written responses she had asked her social studies students to submit so far had revealed some skill deficiencies. She also knew that her students would be called on to write more and more in the high school years ahead and that they would be participating in state-mandated testing again in 10th grade. The writing task they would face then would be interdisciplinary, and student work would be judged against a framework of "writing across the curriculum." In short, although Marcia knew her primary responsibilities were those of a social studies teacher, she also knew that she and her 8th grade colleagues shared responsibility for teaching writing skills—something their students would need throughout the remainder of their schooling and beyond. Would writing skills be an appropriate focus area for her professional development?

Test #1: Essential Teaching and Learning. Writing seemed like an essential area of teaching and learning to Marcia, and to confirm her sense that this was so, she downloaded a copy of her state's K–12 performance standards—the Connecticut Framework K–12 Curricular Goals and Standards (Connecticut State Department of Education, 1998a). She went to the section on written communication ("Producing Texts"), where she read that students should be able to do the following:

- Communicate effectively by determining the appropriate text structure on the basis of audience, purpose, and point of view (p. 61).
- Communicate effectively in descriptive, narrative, expository, and persuasive modes (p. 61).
- Gather, select, organize, and analyze information from primary and secondary sources (p. 62).
- Engage in a process of generating ideas, drafting, revising, editing, and publishing or presenting (p. 62).
- Engage in writing, speaking, and developing visual texts through frequent reflection, reevaluation, and revision (p. 63).

After reviewing these standards, Marcia looked at the state-developed "trace maps" for written communication: more specific learning targets that operationalize the standards to help teachers monitor student performance at identified grade levels. Here, she saw a number of potential targets: slices of teaching and learning that might serve as the foundation for her PBSE professional development plan. Two of these—revising written work and determining audience and point of view—struck Marcia as particularly relevant skills for 8th graders, although she wasn't sure if these were areas of specific need for *her* 8th graders.

Even as Marcia was becoming more intrigued by the idea of focusing on her students' written communication skills, she knew that she was still responsible for ensuring that her students mastered the 8th grade social studies curriculum, including the topic of economic globalization. What she needed to do was clarify how she might incorporate writing instruction into her students' regular assignments. Marcia turned once again to her state standards document, this time looking at the social studies standards (Connecticut State Department of Education, 1998a). In the sections "International Relations" and "Economic Systems," she found several 8th grade standards linked to globalization:

- Describe the organization of the world into nation-states and describe some ways that nation-states interact with each other (p. 159).
- Describe the influence of the United States' political, economic, and cultural ideas on other nations and the influence of other nations on the United States (p. 159).
- Explain how different economic systems (traditional, market, and command) use different means to produce, distribute, and exchange goods and services (p. 168).
- Identify governmental activities that affect the local, state, national, and international economy (p. 168).

• Explain how specialization increases interdependence among producers, consumers, and nations and consequently leads to a higher standard of living (p. 170).

Marcia saw a lot of possibilities in this list of standards. They offered many different ways for her to incorporate writing instruction into the social studies assignments she would create, thus ensuring powerful learning opportunities for both her students and herself. ◿

Test #1 asks, *"Does the target represent an area of essential teaching and learning for the teacher's grade level and content area?"* In Marcia's case, the answer is yes. Both "written communication" and "understanding of economic globalization" appear in her state's standards and in her district's language arts and social studies curricula. She should be confident that her potential focus represents an area of essential teaching and learning.

◿ **Test #2: Schoolwide and District Data.** To confirm that her students needed help with written communication—and to solidify her sense that this essential area of learning was an appropriate target for her professional development objective—Marcia decided to look at how the students at her school had performed on standardized writing tests.

When Marcia acquired the test report from the school guidance counselor, she saw that she would need to organize the data before it could shed light on her students' strengths and weaknesses. She also knew that the standardized test data, which was not broken down by individual student scores, would only give her a picture of how the entire class had scored; she was interested in how well this year's 8th graders had performed in writing relative to other classes of students. She was also curious if this class had shown growth in writing skills over time.

Marcia began by looking at the writing sample subtest of the annual state assessment. It was scored holistically, and the same scoring format and rubric were used from year to year and across grades. Each student's writing sample was scored by two people using a 6-point rubric in which a score of 1 represented inadequate work and a score of 6 indicated commendable performance. The combined ratings of both scorers resulted in aggregate score range of 2 to 12, with a score of 8 considered proficient.

First, Marcia looked at how students from Fairview had scored over the last 4 years, knowing that students in her state had been assessed in grades 4, 6, and 8. To extend the comparison, she included writing sample scores from the elementary school and organized this information into a data table (see Figure 2.1).

Figure 2.1
Fairview Middle School's Average Holistic Writing Score,
Grades 4–8

Year	Grade 4	Grade 6	Grade 8
2003	**7.0**	8.4	8.1
2004	8.1	8.2	8.6
2005	7.8	**7.1**	8.7
2006	7.9	8.3	8.5

Reviewing the data, Marcia was able to quickly note a number of trends:

• This year's 8th graders, when they were in 4th grade (2003) and in 6th grade (2005), had indeed scored lower in writing than other recent classes.

• Other classes had, in general, demonstrated steady improvement in writing from grade 4 to grade 6 and from grade 6 to grade 8.

• This year's 8th graders had demonstrated minimal progress from grades 4 to 6 and remained at performance levels well below those demonstrated by other groups.

This information confirmed that 8th grade students needed help with writing and reinforced Marcia's intention to focus on that area. ◢

Test #2 asks, "*Does an analysis of schoolwide or district performance data suggest that the target is an area needing improvement?*" Again, the answer is yes. When Marcia views the 8th graders' standardized test data analytically, she can see the need for additional instructional intervention in writing.

◢ **Test #3: Classroom Assessments.** Marcia came away from her investigation of standardized test scores convinced that writing was a worthy focus area but with a whole new set of questions. Were all her 8th graders poor writers? If not, what was the distribution of skills across her students? Was there a group of students whose writing skills were so poor that they lowered the average score of the class significantly? Were there specific areas of writing that needed particular attention? To get this information, Marcia reviewed her students' individual performance on 4th and 6th grade standardized assessments. However, she also knew she would need to look at classroom data, and to get that data, she'd need a classroom assessment.

Assessment Creation. Because a writing sample had offered Marcia her first view of student performance, she created a classroom writing assessment of her own, along with a plan to gather performance information that might reveal specific strengths and weakness in writing. Marcia's class had just finished their first full curriculum unit, which happened to focus on a content standard related to globalization and economic independence: "Explain how specialization increases interdependence among producers, consumers, and nations and consequently leads to a higher standard of living" (Connecticut State Department of Education, 1998a, p. 170). Setting out to design her classroom performance assessment of writing, Marcia considered the following factors:

- The content knowledge involved in the task and its relationship to established standards;
- The performance skills to be demonstrated;
- The authenticity of the task as representative of "real-life" knowledge and skills (Wiggins, 1993);
- The elements of quality that she would use to judge the product of the task; and
- The grade-level or other developmental leveling benchmarks against which to compare the work.

Marcia understood that in past years, the 8th grade writing sample subtest had focused on persuasive writing, and that this would likely be the kind of writing her students would be asked to do on the 10th grade integrated writing test. It seemed, then, that persuasive writing skills were integral to the content and performance standards her students needed to master. What's more, Marcia knew her students would certainly need to write persuasively for high school assignments and in real-life situations after graduation. Focusing on a persuasive writing task seemed a clear and compelling direction.

Marcia proceeded to construct a classroom performance assessment that asked her students to write a persuasive essay arguing whether or not the United States should join forces with Japan to gain global control of the electronics industry. She accompanied the prompt with three primary source documents to complement and extend what the students had learned through the unit's class readings and discussions.

Rubric-Based Evaluation. To facilitate the analysis of student work on the classroom assessment, Marcia saw that she needed two rubrics: one for content mastery (already created and used during the unit on specialization) and another for writing skills. For guidelines on this second rubric, she consulted a number of resources: a state-issued handbook identifying the frameworks for state assessments, including specific information on elements of quality for persuasive writing; writing rubrics acquired from language arts teachers at her school; writing textbooks; and Web sites that offered models of writing rubrics and suggestions for using the rubrics effectively (rubicon.com and rubistar.4teachers.org). Ultimately, to ensure that her classroom assessment of writing skills would be aligned with the other performance data she had collected, Marcia decided to use the state's standards for persuasive writing as the foundation for her own rubric. Before administering the writing task, she developed a six-point rubric focused on several aspects of student responses (see Figure 2.2, p. 30).

Marcia also decided that she would examine the performance of only her Period C class. Because all of her classes were grouped heterogeneously, these students would serve as a representative sample of all her 8th graders. To maintain objectivity, she coded these students' papers to conceal their names and enlisted the assistance of an 8th grade language arts colleague to complete the scoring.

When the Period C essays were assessed using the rubric, Marcia plotted the students' scores (see Figure 2.3, p. 31). A score of 4 or higher represented proficiency on each element of persuasive writing; to achieve overall proficiency, students needed to score 4 or higher on all 5 elements of persuasive writing.

Data Analysis. Marcia used three types of analyses to mine the resulting data for specific performance information: *group aggregated data analysis, group disaggregated data analysis,* and *individually disaggregated data analysis.*

Group aggregated data analysis answers the question, "Is there really a problem?" by considering group results from a common assessment. Student performance data showed Marcia that 11 of her 20 students, or 55 percent, fell below proficiency in their overall performance in persuasive writing (see Figure 2.4, p. 32).

Group disaggregated data analysis answers the question, "Where are the specific problem areas?" Looking again at the data on Period C students below proficiency, Marcia could see that they scored particularly low in the area of "Support and Detail" and "Comprehensiveness" (their ability to use all the primary and secondary resources effectively). Marcia hypothesized that the two criteria went hand in hand: students who were unable to support their statements with detail tended to draw less on resource materials. By contrast, the students did fairly well when it came to taking a clear stand for or against a position ("Position"), organizing their thoughts ("Organization"), and communicating clearly and fluently ("Fluency").

Marcia was also interested in how her lower-performing students had scored as a group relative to their higher-performing classmates. A group-to-group comparison produced a powerful evidence of the discrepancy in

Figure 2.2
Persuasive Writing Rubic

Trait	6	5	4	3	2	1
Position	Position for or against the issue is clear, consistent, and compelling	Position for or against the issue is almost always clear, consistent, and compelling	Position for or against the issue is generally clear, consistent, and compelling	Position for or against the issue is somewhat clear	Clarity of position for or against the issue is limited	Little or no evidence of a position taken for or against the issue
Support and Detail	Reasons are fully elaborated and well-supported by specific detail	Reasons are almost always elaborated and supported with specific detail	Reasons are generally elaborated and supported by specific detail	Reasons are elaborated in an inconsistent manner with few specific details	Elaboration and detail are limited and general	Reasons are not well-developed; details are few or vague
Comprehensiveness	Response is consistently well-developed and comprehensive	Response is well-developed throughout most of the piece	Response is generally well-developed	Response is minimally developed	Response is limited or under-developed	There is little or no response to the writing task
Organization	Response demonstrates consistently strong and strategic organization	Organization is strong and strategic throughout most of the piece	Generally strong and strategic organization	Minimal evidence of strategic organization	Somewhat disorganized response	Response is too brief to demonstrate organization
Fluency	Consistently fluent response with a clear flow	Fluent response throughout most of the piece	Generally fluent response	Somewhat awkward in wording and flow	Fluency is limited; response is somewhat confusing	Response is awkward and confusing

Figure 2.3

Period C Scores on the Class Assessment of Writing Skills

		Traits			
Student	*Position*	*Support and Detail*	*Comprehen-siveness*	*Organization*	*Fluency*	**Met Proficiency?**
A	5	3	3	4	4	No
B	4	3	3	4	5	No
C	4	4	4	5	5	Yes
D	6	5	5	5	6	Yes
E	4	2	3	4	4	No
F	5	4	4	4	5	Yes
G	5	2	3	4	4	No
H	4	2	3	4	4	No
I	4	3	3	4	5	No
J	6	4	5	5	5	Yes
K	5	2	2	4	4	No
L	4	3	3	4	4	No
M	5	5	5	5	6	Yes
N	6	4	4	5	4	Yes
O	4	?	3	4	4	No
P	5	4	4	5	5	Yes
Q	4	3	3	4	5	No
R	4	2	2	4	4	No
S	5	4	5	5	5	Yes
T	6	5	5	5	5	Yes
Averages	*4.75*	*3.30*	*3.60*	*4.40*	*4.65*	**9 Yes 11 No**

writing skills, especially in the traits of Support and Detail and Compre-hensiveness (see Figure 2.5, p. 32). She also looked at her students' writing skills through one more group lens: the state department of education's levels of performance. Based on each student's average holistic score, she organized all 20 Period C pupils into groups above, at, or below the goal score of 4, and indicated the results in distinct performance bands:

- "Exceeds Proficiency": 4 students (20% of the class)
- "Meets Proficiency": 5 students (25% of the class)
- "Near Proficiency": 11 students (55% of the class)

Figure 2.4

Period C Students Below Proficiency

Student	Position	Support and Detail	Comprehen- siveness	Organization	Fluency
A	5	3	3	4	4
B	4	3	3	4	5
E	4	2	3	4	4
G	5	2	3	4	4
H	4	2	3	4	4
I	4	3	3	4	5
K	5	2	2	4	4
L	4	3	3	4	4
O	4	2	3	4	4
Q	4	3	3	4	5
R	4	2	2	4	4
Averages	**4.27**	**2.45**	**2.82**	**4.00**	**4.27**

Figure 2.5

Group-to-Group Performance Comparison by Trait

Group	Position	Support and Detail	Comprehen- siveness	Organization	Fluency
Students Who Met Proficiency	5.33	4.33	4.56	4.89	5.11
Students Below Proficiency	4.27	**2.45**	**2.82**	4.00	4.27

Finally, there is individually disaggregated data analysis, which answers the questions, "Who are the students having the most problems, and in what areas of learning do these problems lie?" For Marcia, it was clear that the 11 students who did not meet proficiency were having the most trouble, particularly in the identified areas of Support and Detail and Comprehensiveness. The next step for Marcia was to find out who these students were. She cross-referenced their coded papers with a class list and produced a list of the students who were most in need of instructional intervention in writing (see Figure 2.6). ◪

Figure 2.6
Students Identified for Persuasive Writing Intervention

Student	Position	Support and Detail	Comprehen-siveness	Organization	Fluency
A. Maggie	5	3	3	4	4
B. George	4	3	3	4	5
E. Miguel	4	2	3	4	4
G. Tanya	5	2	3	4	4
H. Zachary	4	2	3	4	4
I. Ethan	4	3	3	4	5
K. Matt	5	2	2	4	4
L. Jasmine	4	3	3	4	4
O. Jim	4	2	3	4	4
Q. Candace	4	3	3	4	5
R. Jose	4	2	2	4	4
Averages	**4.27**	**2.45**	**2.82**	**4.00**	**4.27**

Test #3 asks, *"Does an analysis of classroom assessment data confirm the target as an area needing improvement?"* Marcia's examination of student performance on a diagnostic classroom assessment, backed with a rubric based on state standards, indicates that the answer is yes. Here, Marcia solidifies her decision to focus on persuasive writing and even narrows that focus further to two very specific areas of need: supporting and elaborating arguments and using resources effectively.

◪ **Test #4: The School and District Improvement Plan.** Before making a final determination regarding her proposed focus, Marcia had one last test to perform. Student performance in written communication, particularly persuasive writing, certainly stood out as a critical issue to her, but was it a priority for her school and district? The recent inservice program on Performance-Based Supervision and Evaluation had stressed that much of the model's power resides in the alignment of energy and focus on common and essential goals for student learning. To determine the degree of alignment, Marcia reviewed her district's strategic plan, as well as her school's improvement plan.

The first strategy identified in the district strategic plan read as follows:

Graduates will demonstrate competency in the basic skill areas of communications (reading, writing, listening, and speaking), foreign language, math, science, social science, and technology, which will prepare them for continued learning and the future world of work.

Communication skills also appeared to be a focus of her school's improvement plan, which included this among its goals:

All Fairview Middle School students will meet or exceed high academic content standards and demonstrate academic growth in communication skills, including reading, writing, speaking, and critical viewing. ◪

Test #4 asks, *"Does the target correspond to an area of emphasis in the district or school's improvement plan?"* In Marcia's case, the answer is clearly yes: writing skills are a priority for her school and her district.

◪ With the four tests now complete, Marcia found she was ready to draft a student learning objective:

By May 1 of this academic year, students in my Period C social studies class who scored in the Near Proficiency range (holistic score of 3.0–3.9) on the October writing sample will score in the Proficient or Exceeds Proficient range by demonstrating improvement in Support and Detail and Comprehensiveness in persuasive writing related to the social studies curriculum. ◪

Preparing for Action

Here is a summary of how teachers can apply the four tests to identify the critical "slice" of teaching and learning that will be their improvement objective and the basis for their professional development plan within Performance-Based Supervision and Evaluation:

1. Select a potential area of essential teaching and learning for the grade level and content area, suggested by initial student information or performance data.

2. Gather and analyze schoolwide or district student performance data in multiple ways to discover learning needs within that area.

3. Create, administer, and analyze classroom assessments to confirm the learning needs and narrow the target.

4. Confirm that the potential target corresponds to an area of emphasis in the district or school's improvement plan.

─────────── ▽ KEYSTONE ───────────

The process of "preparing to target improvement" engages teachers in work that is meaningful and invigorating. It encourages them to take an active leadership role in designing professional development plans that help them acquire what they need to know in order to address specific and targeted student learning needs. Moreover, this process results in a major change in both the supervision and evaluation paradigm by shifting the relationship between the teacher and the supervisor from one primarily led by the supervisor to one in which the teacher takes the lead to improve student learning.

3

Working Together to
Initiate Teacher Development

◪ The clock in Gary Mulholland's office read 9:10 a.m.—just five minutes until his first appointment with staff members to begin the work of creating individual professional development plans based on student learning needs. It was early October, and today, Gary was set to meet with three teachers: 8th grade social studies teacher Marcia Williams, 7th grade math teacher Eileen Blanchard, and physical education teacher Larry Rinaldi.

Gary had worked hard to lay the foundation for these meetings. He had discussed Performance-Based Supervision and Evaluation at the May and June faculty meetings and had distributed reading materials for teachers to review before the new school year began. Just prior to opening day, Fairview teachers had participated in two full days of professional development on PBSE, followed by four after-school seminars for further discussion. And two weeks ago, in mid-September, he had sent out a memo reminding all teachers to set up an appointment to discuss their students' performance and their ideas about a potential professional development goal. He asked that each faculty member begin to think about the "four tests" they'd need to conduct as part of their preparation and bring to the meeting some evidence of student performance that might provide a potential basis for their professional development focus.

Gary's first appointment was with Eileen Blanchard, a 7th grade math teacher. She entered the room carrying a slim manila folder and her grade book.

"I saw your memo," Eileen began. "There was something about student work, but I wasn't sure what you wanted, and I thought this meeting was about my professional development plan, anyway. I've brought my grade book and the last set of quizzes I gave to my Period B pre-algebra

36

class. I don't think the quizzes will be very helpful, though, because it's the beginning of the year and most of what the students are doing now is review."

It was becoming clear to Gary that Eileen was "data anemic": she didn't collect much performance data on her students beyond what she recorded in her grade book, she was generally inexperienced with data analysis, and she was unsure how to use student performance data to inform her instructional plans. Gary quickly realized that before he and Eileen could begin to talk about her professional development focus, he'd need to provide her with support and coaching to help her develop a clearer understanding of the PBSE model.

Physical education teacher Larry Rinaldi stepped into Gary's office at precisely 11:50 a.m. He toted a box filled with file folders, several video-tapes, and his grade book.

"I'm pretty excited about this new model of supervision and evalua-tion," Larry said. "As you know, the physical education department here at Fairview has led the way when it comes to collecting and reporting student performance data. The kids take a number of tests each year for the state physical fitness assessment, but PE staff members here go way beyond that. We have several years' worth of performance data on file so that we can look at progress over time. That includes videotaped per-formance, which we use in conferencing with our students and parents about fitness. We also issue progress reports for 6th and 7th graders, which focus on the major areas of our curriculum, and we computerized these reports three years ago to make it easier to track growth. I also brought all of the information I've collected on my PE students this year. I know it's a lot," Larry said, smiling, "but in PE, we see all the kids in the school all the time, and I didn't know where to begin."

Gary took a deep breath, knowing right away that, unlike Eileen, Larry was "data prolific." He was enthusiastic, that was certain, and he had lots and lots of data. But apart from collecting and archiving this information, Larry had little knowledge about or experience with analyzing the data, looking at it from a variety of perspectives, or cutting through the paper-work to prioritize instructional interventions. Gary understood that Larry would need significant help zeroing in on a single slice of teaching and learning as the basis for his professional development plan.

As Marcia Williams entered Gary's office, he felt a sense of encour-agement. Her demeanor was enthusiastic, and she carried what appeared to be organized files of reasonable size. After presenting a thorough analysis of student performance data, Marcia slid a single sheet of paper toward him. On it was a brief statement:

> By May 1 of this academic year, students in my Period C social studies class who scored in the Near Proficiency range (holistic score of 3.0–3.9) on the October writing sample will score in the Proficient or Exceeds Proficient range by demonstrating improvement in Support and Detail and Comprehensiveness in persuasive writing related to the social studies curriculum.

"What do you think?" Marcia asked.

Based on this student learning objective, Gary identified Marcia as "data strategic." He knew that Marcia had understood what Performance-Based Supervision and Evaluation was about, had taken some time to consider her students and their skills, and had worked through the "four tests." He opened the folder Marcia had prepared, and together, they began to pore over the work she'd done to arrive at this point. ◾

Foundational Understandings of the PBSE Process

Teachers and supervisors beginning the actual work of collaborating to improve student learning face three key challenges related to overarching aspects of the model:

1. They must understand different types of data and how each contributes to the kinds of judgments that underlie the PBSE professional development plan.

2. They must grasp that PBSE is a type of applied action research that allows the teacher and supervisor to make informed interventions, monitor the success of these interventions, and adjust the instructional activities that follow.

3. They must commit to high-quality collaboration on behalf of student learning.

Let's take a closer look at each of these aspects.

The Types and Sources of Student Performance Data

In Chapter 2, we illustrated how important the collection and analysis of student performance data were in Marcia Williams's preparation work. In fact, decisions based on these data are so critical to establishing, monitoring, and adjusting an effective PBSE professional development plan that an overview of various data sources is in order. Throughout the duration of the plan, which may take place during one academic year or extend over a longer period, student performance data serve very different purposes. There are four types of data we want to highlight. The first two, *prompting data* and *confirming data,* are particularly useful in the Teacher Preparation Phase of PBSE, when teachers are working to determine a new focus area for their improvement objective.

Prompting Data. A variety of information comes to teachers and other school professionals as they assess learning in their subject areas. Typical sources include

- Standardized or corporate test results.
- Classroom testing and assessment experiences.
- Parent and community input.
- Internal school or district communications about how well students are prepared at various levels (for example, high school teachers' feedback about middle schoolers' preparation).
- University or employer feedback on prerequisite learning requirements for advanced education or jobs.
- Research reports.

This kind of information acts to prompt teachers to begin looking at a potential focus for their work because it points out areas where instructional intervention may be needed. The data also prompt teachers to ask several key questions: *"Can I generalize this information to my own work and my own students? Should I use this information as a rationale to justify a professional development focus for myself—a focus that will serve to improve the learning of my students while also improving my work as a teacher?"*

Confirming Data. Teachers and other school professionals who suspect a problematic learning trend need to develop assessments that establish whether those suspicions are indeed accurate. An effective choice is a holistic or performance-based assessment, developed by the teacher and grounded in relevant district curriculum standards. This kind of assessment provides baseline data that initially confirm that there is a problem and help give that problem some definition, both in terms of content and the individual learning needs of specific students.

Action Research Data. As teachers and other school professionals respond to initial baseline data, they will develop and implement instructional interventions aimed at improving student performance in targeted areas. Much like action researchers use data to inform a change in practice, teachers in the PBSE model continually assess student performance to see if the interventions are making a difference. Follow-up data become true action research data when they are collected cyclically and regularly re-analyzed for the purpose of further modifying teaching to maximize the positive effects on student learning.

Summative Data. This designation applies to data on student performance collected at the chosen end point of an action research cycle. They represent the best evidence of a student's proficiency level at a single point in time—a snapshot of skills and understanding. Remember, though, that designating a final assessment and resultant data as "summative" does not preclude a continuation of the action research cycle.

The Action Research Connection

From a broad perspective, the PBSE professional development plan is analogous to what is commonly known as action research, and as such, it lays out a process similar to the scientific method.

• Like *asking a question or posing a problem,* the teacher's focus for improving student learning clarifies and drives the teacher's professional development and related investigation.

• When the teacher and supervisor agree on which instructional interventions will be implemented, they are *hypothesizing* potential solutions to the problem.

- The chosen instructional interventions become the *treatment* applied to improve student learning.
- Once instructional interventions have taken place, additional *data are collected* to measure student progress from the baseline.
- These data give rise to *conclusions* about the efficacy of the instructional interventions: are they improving student performance?

The quality of the PBSE model as action research depends on consistent and timely decisions and actions throughout the inquiry process. The teacher and supervisor must commit to collecting valid, high-quality data before, during, and after instruction. And they must work together to make meaning of the resulting student performance information and determine the most effective subsequent interventions.

The Power of Committed Collaboration

Generally speaking, most of us enjoy working with others and feel that we accomplish more when we do. Cognitive learning theory posits an explanation. The work of Lev S. Vygotsky, conducted during the early 1900s but gaining increasing attention and support over the past decade, asserts that the social environment is critical for learning. At the heart of Vygotsky's theory is a concept known as the "zone of proximal development," which emphasizes that we learn best when guided by a mentor or collaborating with a more experienced peer (Schunk, 2000).

Collaboration's importance within the learning environment emerged more recently in a study commissioned by the Governance Board of the National Research Council. The project produced a meta-analysis of recent research on how learning takes place and offered suggestions for applying these findings in classroom practice. Published in 2000, the comprehensive report *How People Learn: Brain, Mind, Experience, and School* (Bransford, Brown, & Cocking, 2000) takes the position that what is known about effective learning applies to teachers as well as their students. The study identified four characteristics of highly effective learning environments:

1. They are *learner-centered,* building on the strengths, interests, and needs of the learner.

2. They are *knowledge-centered,* offering well-organized knowledge that supports understanding.

3. They are *assessment-centered,* offering learners an opportunity to test their understanding by trying things out and getting feedback.

4. They are *community-centered,* developing cultural norms and encouraging collaboration in order to support learning.

The professional literature on developing and maintaining teacher quality is also replete with calls to improve teaching environments. The logic in these recommendations is that teachers who feel that their workplace supports their professional endeavors and nurtures their collaborative efforts will develop increased efficacy, and this will have a positive effect on student learning (Hall & Hord, 2001).

The kind of collaborative professional environment most often discussed in the literature is *teacher-to-teacher* collaboration. Peer coaching, action research projects, team teaching, middle school teams, and the like all bring classroom teachers together to support and extend each other's work. Another well-known extension of teacher-to-teacher collaboration is the *professional learning community model,* a design in which all members of a school community collaborate toward a shared mission: student learning (DuFour & Eaker, 1998; Glickman, Gordon, & Ross-Gordon, 2004; Hord, 1997).

This broader view of collaboration offers an appropriate context for understanding a powerful feature of Performance-Based Supervision and Evaluation: its primary collaboration is between *teacher and supervisor,* not teacher and teacher. In PBSE, although the collaboration between an administrator and a teacher is much like cognitive coaching (Costa & Garmston, 1985), their partnership serves two additional, specific purposes: to guide the teacher to be more analytical about student work, and to prepare the teacher to create a professional development plan.

──────────────── ▽ KEYSTONE ────────────────

In contrast to traditional teacher supervision and evaluation, the richness of the PBSE model lies in the conversation between the teacher and supervisor as they collaborate to enhance the teacher's instructional capacity to improve student learning in essential knowledge, skills, and dispositions.

Monitoring the Process: The Criteria of Excellence

So, how should a collaborative administrator respond to and coach the three Fairview Middle School teachers and their colleagues? Our model of Performance-Based Supervision and Evaluation offers explicit guidelines in the form of the Criteria of Excellence (see Appendix A). As outlined in Chapter 1, the Criteria are organized in six phases and present specific indicators of progress spelling out what teachers should know and be able to do in order to continue becoming "smarter" about improving student learning. Collectively, they represent a single, well-defined continuum of growth—a path focused on improving student performance, but built on the understanding that individual teachers will be walking it at different paces and at different times.

Within our model, the unique and deep understanding of what it means to be truly *performance based* comes alive in the Criteria's sequence of skills, behaviors, and accomplishments for teachers and their supervisors. Educators do not simply *think* they know where they are in their progress; they use evidence to delineate where they *actually* are. The Criteria provide a way to plot teachers' growing capacity for collecting and analyzing student work, for using that information to plan instructional interventions, and for identifying and acquiring the kind of appropriate professional development that will enable them to do this more effectively.

A Review of the Phases

A brief review of the Criteria phases informs our continuing discussion of this supervision management tool.

The Teacher Preparation Phase. The teacher launches the PBSE process by identifying student performance data related to essential learning and completes a preliminary analysis of these data. In Chapter 2, we saw Marcia do this.

The Initial Collaboration Phase. The teacher and supervisor discuss the teacher's preliminary performance data analysis, agree on the objective for improving student learning, draft a professional development plan, and agree on related supervisory activities.

The Initial Monitoring Phase. The teacher embarks on the individual professional development plan to acquire new professional learning that will support strategic instructional interventions for students. This phase incorporates clear and ongoing communication between the teacher and supervisor.

The Mid-Cycle Review Phase. The teacher and supervisor meet to discuss progress to date and, if necessary, revise both the teacher's development plan and related monitoring and support activities. Artifacts from the teacher's initiatives, from student work, and from the supervisor's activities offer both accountability and real data to inform the review.

The Secondary Monitoring Phase. The teacher continues with professional development, instructional interventions, and analysis of performance data, with some plans and procedures modified based on the outcome of the mid-cycle review. The supervisor offers continued monitoring and support, adjusted based on review findings.

The Summative Review Phase. The teacher and supervisor meet for a final review of the teacher's work before the end of the teacher growth cycle. As in traditional summative conferences, this meeting includes reflection about the work done throughout the year as well as written reports of accomplishments.

Using the Criteria to Monitor Progress

When using the Criteria to monitor teachers' progress, supervisors might simply check off individual indicators as the teacher accomplishes them, or they might use the evaluation scale included on the forms to describe more specifically the teacher's level of accomplishment: "C" indicates that the teacher has completed the activity or achieved competence in the necessary skills; "E" indicates that the activity is in progress, or the skills are emergent; and "JB" indicates that work on the activity or the skills is just beginning. We have found this rating scale to be a simple but effective tool. Used in this way, the Criteria offer a clear picture of each teacher's status in regard to developing competencies. In addition, when supervisors look at the progress all teachers have made, the Criteria give a collective picture of the growing instructional capacity of the entire faculty.

Using the Criteria of Excellence to Determine a Teacher's Starting Point

As we have seen in preceding vignettes, the teachers at Fairview Middle School are working in the Teacher Preparation Phase of the PBSE process, albeit at different rates and with varied levels of understanding. Principal Gary Mulholland can use the specific indicators associated with this phase (see Figure 3.1, p. 46) to plan his collaboration with each teacher.

Another look at Marcia and her colleagues Eileen and Larry illustrates the multiple ways in which administrators can differentiate the start of the PBSE process.

Figure 3.1
Criteria of Excellence for the Teacher Preparation Phase

Indicator	Criteria
TP-1 _____ TP-2 _____	*The teacher has identified* • Student performance data that represent "essential learning" and are standards-based. • Student performance data that result from holistic assessment of a learning task requiring students to apply multiple skills and various knowledge.
TP-3 _____ TP-4 _____	*The teacher has organized* • Student performance data so that they may be viewed and interpreted in more than one way. • Student performance data to reveal student performance strengths and weaknesses.
TP-5 _____ TP-6 _____ TP-7 _____	*The teacher has completed an analysis of data, producing* • Some conclusions about student performance strengths and weaknesses. • Some artifacts of student work exemplifying student performance strengths and weaknesses. • Some ideas about how to modify teaching to bring about improved student learning in the areas targeted in the data analysis.

Evaluation Scale: C = Competent; E = Emergent; JB = Just Beginning

Initiating the Process with the Data-Anemic Teacher

You will recall that Eileen Blanchard, our 7th grade math teacher, showed up for her first meeting with the principal with just a grade book and a handful of quizzes. Figure 3.2 shows Gary's notes about

Figure 3.2
Eileen Blanchard's Teacher Preparation Phase Status—October

Indicator	Criteria
TP-1 __E__ **Start!** TP-2 __JB__	*The teacher has identified* • Student performance data that represent "essential learning" and are standards-based. • Student performance data that result from holistic assessment of a learning task requiring students to apply multiple skills and various knowledge.
TP-3 __JB__ TP-4 __JB__	*The teacher has organized* • Student performance data so that they may be viewed and interpreted in more than one way. • Student performance data to reveal student performance strengths and weaknesses.
TP-5 __JB__ TP-6 __JB__ TP-7 __JB__	*The teacher has completed an analysis of data, producing* • Some conclusions about student performance strengths and weaknesses. • Some artifacts of student work exemplifying student performance strengths and weaknesses. • Some ideas about how to modify teaching to bring about improved student learning in the areas targeted in the data analysis.
Evaluation Scale: C = Competent; E = Emergent; JB = Just Beginning	

her progress to date on the Criteria of Excellence for the Teacher Preparation Phase.

With Eileen—a teacher who is quite inexperienced with data gathering and analysis—Gary's first challenge is to help her focus on student performance and learn how to use performance data more strategically. Overall, he will need to craft a slow, steady, and sensitive coaching plan to support her professional development within the PBSE process. Before Eileen can begin to address her students' learning needs, she must first focus on her own developmental needs.

Gary and Eileen's collaboration will begin with a series of meetings to discuss specific topics related to student performance, district standards, and essential learning. Between these sessions, Eileen will be responsible for gathering additional information for the next discussion. To illustrate, Gary might schedule several conversations with Eileen to do the following:

1. Help Eileen to identify three or four 7th grade mathematics units that her students typically find difficult.

2. Connect Eileen's perceptions of these "difficult units" to some form of data—even the contents of her grade book. What student performance data indicate areas of difficulty?

3. Examine Eileen's students' performance on last year's 6th grade standardized test in mathematics. Do any areas of lower performance correlate with the knowledge and skills addressed in the difficult units Eileen has identified?

4. Review the performance of Fairview Middle School students on last year's 8th grade standardized mathematics test. Where are the scores low? Do these areas overlap with the areas of lower performance on last year's 6th grade test or in Eileen's difficult units?

5. Examine the relationship between the difficult units and the district standards articulated in the curriculum. How are the district's math standards reflected in the content of Eileen's instruction?

6. Identify the essential learning represented in the standardized tests Eileen's students will take in 8th grade. What do students need to learn so that they will have the knowledge and skills that the state has deemed critical?

The goal for Eileen and Gary's collaborative preparation is to synthesize the prompting data that Eileen collects, make connections within this information, and gradually zero-in on a specific area of student performance: one that represents essential learning, district priorities, and student performance needs. It is only after this "prep work" is complete that they will be able to discuss and then agree on an improvement objective and the kind of professional development Eileen will need to address her students' learning needs most effectively.

When will Eileen move on to creating a professional development plan framed by the PBSE model? The answer depends on her. Some teachers need an entire school year to focus on just the first few Criteria of Excellence, such as an increased focus on student performance data (TP-1) or the development of more performance-based assessments to create richer student assessment data (TP-2). Once these teachers have learned to apply these skills with consistency and confidence, they will have the foundation they need to progress toward full PBSE implementation. More detailed discussion of Eileen and Gary's collaborative journey continues in the chapters ahead.

Initiating the Process with the Data-Prolific Teacher

Physical education teacher Larry Rinaldi is already committed to using student performance data to monitor progress and communicate growth. His many assessment initiatives attest to his strong belief in data collection, and he is very familiar with the state physical education assessments he administers each year. However, in Gary's judgment, Larry is not as familiar with how to use data strategically to plan instructional interventions. Figure 3.3 (see p. 50) shows Gary's assessment of Larry's status within the Teacher Preparation Phase of the Criteria of Excellence.

Gary's first challenge with Larry is to help him cut through the mountain of data and identify which understandings are truly "essential" for his students. Larry has plenty of classroom data, but Gary needs to prompt him to look first at state assessments as

Figure 3.3
Larry Rinaldi's Teacher Preparation Phase Status—October

Indicator	Criteria
TP-1 __C__ TP-2 __C__	*The teacher has identified* • Student performance data that represent "essential learning" and are standards-based. • Student performance data that result from holistic assessment of a learning task requiring students to apply multiple skills and various knowledge.
TP-3 __E__ **Start!** TP-4 __E__	*The teacher has organized* • Student performance data so that they may be viewed and interpreted in more than one way. • Student performance data to reveal student performance strengths and weaknesses.
TP-5 __E__ TP-6 __E__ TP-7 __JB__	*The teacher has completed an analysis of data, producing* • Some conclusions about student performance strengths and weaknesses. • Some artifacts of student work exemplifying student performance strengths and weaknesses. • Some ideas about how to modify teaching to bring about improved student learning in the areas targeted in the data analysis.
Evaluation Scale: C = Competent; E = Emergent; JB = Just Beginning	

a way to identify a narrow, deep, and significant area of learning within the physical education program.

Gary might schedule some conversations with Larry to help him do the following:

1. Identify and understand the standards represented on the state physical fitness test. What knowledge and skills does the state

value as essential learning? What will students need to know and be able to do for this assessment?

2. Pull together student performance data on state assessments across grade levels and within specific areas of knowledge or skills. What were the results on each component of the test for aggregate groups of students? Is there an area of student performance that raises concern?

3. Examine classroom data and Larry's perceptions regarding his students' performance. What insight can his current classroom assessment data provide? Are there areas of lower performance within the physical education curriculum that correlate with areas of lower performance on the state assessment?

4. Craft additional classroom assessments to acquire confirming data: additional baseline data and insight into his students' current skill levels.

Given Larry's enthusiasm for and experience with data collection and performance monitoring, it seems likely that with continuing but judicious supervision, he will soon be ready to create a professional development plan that includes the essential elements of the PBSE model. Larry's story continues in more detail in the chapters that follow.

Initiating the Process with the Data-Strategic Teacher

To borrow a phrase from a familiar children's story, Marcia Williams's first efforts to use the PBSE model to chart a course for improved student learning were "just right." Figure 3.4 (see p. 52) shows Gary's notes about her progress to date on the Criteria of Excellence for the Teacher Preparation Phase. In Gary's judgment—which is based on the artifacts Marcia has developed during her investigations and new learning as well as on her ability to discuss this work with clear depth of understanding and professional reflection—she has achieved basic competency in all the phase's indicators.

Figure 3.4
Marcia Williams's Teacher Preparation Phase Status—October

Indicator	Criteria
TP-1 __C__ TP-2 __C__	*The teacher has identified* • Student performance data that represent "essential learning" and are standards-based. • Student performance data that result from holistic assessment of a learning task requiring students to apply multiple skills and various knowledge.
TP-3 __C__ TP-4 __C__	*The teacher has organized* • Student performance data so that they may be viewed and interpreted in more than one way. • Student performance data to reveal student performance strengths and weaknesses.
TP-5 __C__ TP-6 __C__ TP-7 __C__	*The teacher has completed an analysis of data, producing* • Some conclusions about student performance strengths and weaknesses. • Some artifacts of student work exemplifying student performance strengths and weaknesses. • Some ideas about how to modify teaching to bring about improved student learning in the areas targeted in the data analysis.

Evaluation Scale: C = Competent; E = Emergent; JB = Just Beginning

Getting started with a data-strategic teacher like Marcia is a matter of building on a solid foundation. Gary's plan for Marcia is to move fairly quickly to the Initial Collaboration Phase of the PBSE model, where both principal and teacher focus on the teacher's professional development plan: her ideas for improving performance and the attendant professional development she will need to acquire the knowledge and skills that will support informed instructional interventions. In the meantime, given Marcia's social studies orientation, Gary might recommend that she do the following:

1. Self-assess her skills as a teacher of writing.

2. Begin to seek out resources that will help her increase her own capacity and skill in written expression. Gary's and Marcia's colleagues who teach writing could be excellent resources, as could district curriculum specialists.

Individual Paths to Teacher Preparation

Performance-Based Supervision and Evaluation offers a framework for synthesizing best practice around student learning that is flexible enough to be effective with all teachers. Marcia, with her quick grasp of the PBSE model and instinctual navigations of the four tests depicted in Chapter 2, offers a portrait of a teacher with solid instructional skills, openness to new processes, an affinity for data analysis, and the confidence and ability to absorb new professional learning and apply it fairly independently. Eileen and Larry present somewhat different pictures, and they help to illustrate the range of data-analysis experience and skills that exist within a typical faculty. However, as the continuation of our teachers' journeys will clarify, the PBSE process provides the means for all teachers to increase their instructional capacity and improve student learning, regardless of where they begin on the path or how quickly they travel it.

4

Creating Individual
Professional Development Plans

Professional development plans within the PBSE model are consistent with the best principles of action research and contribute to the conversation deep at the heart of a professional learning community. They are developed by teachers with input from supervisors; oriented toward boosting student achievement; current and authentic, in that they are built on actual student needs as demonstrated by data; and achievable within the scope of a teacher's professional responsibilities.

Although each teacher's professional development plan is unique and grounded in the teacher's analysis of student performance data, all PBSE professional development plans share some common characteristics:

• They spell out what the teacher needs to know to guide students toward improved achievement in the targeted area of learning.

• They embed opportunities for the supervisor and other colleagues to be involved in the teacher's professional development, with roles differentiated to support the teacher's needs.

• They build in time for the teacher and supervisor to have additional, rich conversations around classroom assessments.

• They target specific initiatives the teacher will undertake to improve student learning and monitor the effects of those initiatives.

Putting a Plan Together

The Criteria of Excellence for the Initial Collaboration Phase provide indicators to guide the teacher's work to draft a professional development plan and give the supervisor a roadmap for what's to be done (see Figure 4.1, p. 56).

The teacher's first draft of the plan is based on the focus that emerges during preparation activities: reflection on essential learning and the analysis of student work, various student performance data, and the goals of the district and school improvement plans. Beginning with that focus, and working collaboratively with the administrator, the teacher does the following:

1. Makes a written commitment to improvement in this area by establishing an improvement objective that is based on student learning.

2. Develops specific, research- and standards-based indicators that will show that students are making progress toward the objective.

3. Creates a two-part action plan that describes what the teacher will do throughout the year for the students (the instructional interventions) and what the teacher will do for herself to increase her knowledge and instructional capacity.

Crafting an effective professional development plan is the cornerstone of the PBSE model. The plan is what holds the process together, allowing both the teacher and supervisor to keep track of their activities and monitor progress. That said, the plan also needs to offer enough flexibility so that both the teacher and supervisor can make modifications along the way to further support student learning.

Figure 4.1
Criteria of Excellence for the Initial Collaboration Phase

Indicator	Criteria
	The teacher and supervisor have had conversation(s) producing
IC-1 _____	• A review of the teacher's initial data analysis and conclusions or ideas for improvement.
IC-2 _____	• Some expansion and extension of the teacher's initial data analysis.
IC-3 _____	• Some brainstorming of the elements of a professional development plan that is responsive to the data analysis.
IC-4 _____	• Some brainstorming of the elements of a professional development plan designed to support the teacher's efforts to improve (ideas for "getting smarter" and increasing capacity).
	The teacher and supervisor have agreed on
IC-5 _____	• A formal and detailed teacher improvement objective with a chronology of processes and outcomes stated in student-performance terms. This objective is developed by the teacher.
IC-6 _____	• A formal and detailed professional development plan crafted by the teacher.
IC-7 _____	• A general identification and description of the supervisory activities (observations, conferences, reviews of student work, etc.) to take place during the Initial Monitoring Phase.

Evaluation Scale: C = Competent; E = Emergent; JB = Just Beginning

──────────── ▽ KEYSTONE ────────────

The PBSE professional development plan represents a commitment to improving student performance and serves as an important tool to put into practice interventions that the teacher and supervisor believe will most effectively improve student learning.

How does it all come together? Again, we will use the example of our 8th grade social studies teacher, Marcia Williams, to illustrate how this process evolves, albeit somewhat ideally, in practice.

◢ In Gary's judgment, Marcia had completed the necessary preparation work (see Figure 3.4) and was ready to move on to the next phase of the PBSE process, the heart of which was the development of a professional development plan. Over the next few weeks, Gary would use the Criteria of Excellence for the Initial Collaboration Phase to guide the work he and Marcia would do together. They would make more definitive decisions about the data analysis and specific focus for improving student learning and agree on a professional development plan that would help Marcia address her students' needs. Based on this, Gary would decide on the supervisory initiatives that would best support Marcia's endeavors. ◢

Reviewing the Teacher's Data Analysis and Confirming the Student Learning Objective

To create a relevant professional development plan, one of the first things a teacher and supervisor will do is review and discuss prompting and confirming data. The goal is to affirm that the teacher is focusing on an area of essential learning where instructional intervention is warranted.

◢ Using the data tables she had created, Marcia showed Gary how she had analyzed student performance data in several ways to "drill down" and uncover specific areas of writing where some of her students need additional support and instruction. She explained how she had identified her focus area (writing) and narrowed the improvement objective to the following:

By May 1 of this academic year, students in my Period C social studies class who scored in the Near Proficiency range (holistic score of 3.0–3.9) on the October writing sample will score in the Proficient or Exceeds Proficient range by demonstrating improvement in Support and Detail and Comprehensiveness in persuasive writing related to the social studies curriculum.

While reviewing Marcia's student learning objective, Gary noted a number of key features:

- The objective was inspired by student (*confirming*) performance data and the goals of the school improvement plan.
- It focused on student performance rather than on teacher activities.
- It clearly identified the target population for instructional intervention.
- It specified the narrow area of essential learning to be addressed.
- It detailed the desired level of improved performance and the time frame for both the baseline and post-intervention assessment.

With a clear, narrow, and appropriate objective in place, Marcia and Gary agreed that they were ready to move to the next step. ◪

Setting Indicators to Measure Student Learning Progress

How will a teacher know if student learning is improving in the focus area? There must be clear "mile markers" to measure students' progress toward the objective. These indicators are developed by the teacher and formalized through discussion with the supervisor.

◪ For indicators, Marcia and Gary focused on the conclusions Marcia had derived from her data analysis. In Marcia's Period C class, 11 students fell in the Near Proficient range when their persuasive writing samples were scored holistically. However, when their work was viewed using a more analytic approach, it became apparent that they had much lower degrees of understanding and application ability in the areas of Support and Detail and Comprehensiveness. Marcia and Gary determined that if Marcia's instructional interventions were to be deemed effective, her target students would need to demonstrate measurable growth in these two critical areas. They also decided that Marcia would need to develop additional performance assessments appropriate to the indicators as post-intervention measures.

For specific indicators of progress, Marcia drafted the following:

When their May content-grounded writing sample is analyzed for both Support and Detail and Comprehensiveness targeted students will demonstrate improvement in persuasive writing by scoring 4 or higher as measured by the persuasive writing rubric.

To ensure that her assessments would be reliable and valid measures of her students' learning relative to the content standards for persuasive writing, Marcia planned to use the same rubric to judge student responses to writing prompts throughout the year—the six-point rubric she had constructed based on state curriculum standards (see Figure 2.2). She also planned to assess her students' writing skills regularly, so that she could modify her interventions if students were not making sufficient progress. And because Marcia's background was in social studies, not writing, she decided that most of her own learning for the year would focus on writing instruction and on developing additional standards-based tools to assess student writing in her content area. ◢

Creating a Two-Part Action Plan

A professional development plan within the PBSE model considers dual initiatives: instructional activities to directly affect student learning and professional development activities to increase the teacher's capacity to implement the instructional activities.

◢ At Gary's suggestion, Marcia drafted a professional development plan using a common time line to synchronize both of its aspects: her learning and the interventions she planned for her students. The plan she put together (see Figure 4.2, p. 60) included everything she had done in the preceding month and what she would do for the remainder of the school year, as well as what would be happening for Marcia's students. ◢

Planning for Ongoing Monitoring and Support

As the professional development plan comes together, the supervisor reflects on the nature of the teacher's work with students and makes a note of where the teacher seems to be along the continuum of the Criteria of Excellence. In addition, the supervisor begins to assist the teacher in acquiring the resources needed to support the teacher's new learning. As the teacher pursues the plan, she and

Figure 4.2
A Model Professional Development Plan for Improving Persuasive Writing

Plan for the Students	Time Line	Plan for the Teacher
	by September 15	• Investigate state standards for writing, especially persuasive writing. • Contact the building writing expert to seek support in developing an assessment to collect confirming data.
	by October 1	• Develop a writing assessment instrument for baseline data. • Develop a standards-based rubric for the assessment. • Sign up for the fall districtwide inservice course on standards-based writing instruction.
• Administer a baseline writing assessment.	by October 10	• Continue to investigate PD resources for writing instruction and assessment.
	by October 20	• Complete an analysis of the baseline assessment; identify the group of students for intervention. • Ask the building writing expert for informal coaching on writing instruction and assessment. • Begin the fall districtwide inservice course on standards-based writing instruction.
	by October 30	○ Complete a teacher–supervisor review of student performance data and discuss the focus of the professional development plan.
	by October 31	• Complete an initial search for PD resources; acquire resource materials (books, articles, guides, etc.) for teaching and assessing the writing skills of elaboration and comprehensiveness, particularly in persuasive writing. ○ Complete a draft professional development plan.
	by November 15	• Review acquired resource materials and complete draft lesson plans for instructional interventions. • Review and revise these lesson plans with supervisor.

• Begin implementing intervention lessons with a focus on elaboration and comprehensiveness in persuasive writing with the target group of students.	by November 20	• Continue participation in the district inservice course on standards-based writing instruction.
	by January 5	• Develop an intermediate assessment to be used with the previously developed persuasive writing rubric.
• Administer an intermediate writing assessment to the intervention group, focusing on elaboration and comprehensiveness.	by January 15	○ Update list of PD resources related to elaboration and comprehensiveness in persuasive writing. • Sign up for the district's spring course on standards-based assessment.
	by January 20	• Analyze and review the intermediate writing assessment; make necessary changes to instructional interventions.
• Continue instructional interventions for elaboration and comprehensiveness in persuasive writing, modified based on analysis of the performance data.	by February 1	• Submit a mid-cycle report of progress in student learning to supervisor. ○ Complete the mid-cycle conference with supervisor; modify professional development plan as needed. • Begin district course on standards-based assessment.
	by April 15	○ Schedule and complete the supervisor's observation of intervention lessons, teacher–supervisor post-observation conferencing, and instructional adjustments.
• Administer a summative writing assessment to intervention group. • Ask involved students to write a personal reflection about their learning as a member of the intervention group.	by May 1	○ Complete readings, consultations with writing experts, and other PD activities.
	by May 5	• Complete an analysis and review of summative assessment data, including student comments.
	by May 20	○ Submit results and a final report of progress to supervisor. • Schedule and complete the summative conference and reflect on the year's professional development plan.

○ Open bullets indicate activities reflective of more traditional models of supervision and evaluation.

her supervisor will schedule classroom observations, meetings to discuss student work, or any other activities requiring their direct collaboration. The Criteria of Excellence for the Initial Monitoring Phase provide the means for monitoring the teacher's progress.

A Closer Look at a Model PBSE Professional Development Plan

Notice that Marcia's PBSE-guided professional development plan includes many activities typically associated with traditional supervision and evaluation processes, such as beginning-, middle-, and end-of-year conferences, as well as supervisory classroom observations. The integration is purposeful, to demonstrate how the PBSE model can fit into any pre-existing expectation for teacher supervision and evaluation. However, within PBSE, the work done by teachers and their supervisors derives from an analytic investigation of student learning needs in essential content areas.

For Marcia and her students, this means focusing on standards-based knowledge and skills in need of improvement. From this investigation, the teacher takes the lead in identifying a "slice" of student performance as the focus for her own learning. The professional development related to this slice of essential learning increases the teacher's capacity to address the instructional needs of many students after her work with the target intervention group has been completed. As Marcia becomes more knowledgeable about strengthening the writing skills of her target students, she naturally uses her new learning to help all of her students become more effective writers. Throughout the cycle, the supervisor's work is to act as a "critical friend" to support the teacher's learning relative to this slice of essential learning. In our scenario, Gary will work closely with Marcia to review her progress and make strategic suggestions for further professional growth. Most important, the supervisor's classroom observations are focused on lessons related to the teacher's improvement objective. This gives the supervisor an opportunity to see instructional interventions in action and provide feedback that will inform the teacher's further professional development and future instruction. In Gary's case, he will want to observe lessons that demonstrate Marcia's growing knowledge of writing instruction and to discuss with her the impact that this knowledge has had on classroom instruction and student learning.

Marcia's plan also illustrates her effort to explore a variety of internal and external resources to support her professional development. Although the typical array of readings, conferences, and support materials do nurture teacher learning, these are often "one time" experiences without clear and continuing links to actual classroom instruction. The "internal" supports found in one's own school and district are often more enduring and connected. In her plan, Marcia identifies a colleague (the school's writing coordinator) as one source of internal support and ongoing district inservice courses addressing writing instruction and standards-based assessment as another.

Finally, note that although Marcia's professional development plan spans one academic year, the significant work of improving teacher capacity to improve student learning often demands a longer time frame. Depending on the area of essential learning and target population of students, professional development plans may require two or more years of intervention and capacity-building activities.

—————————— ▽ KEYSTONE ——————————

The PBSE professional development plan integrates with more traditional formats for district supervision and evaluation. Targeting specific instructional interventions to increase student learning in essential areas of knowledge and skills dovetails with a system of collegial conferencing and classroom observations to provide a clear focus for the work of both the teacher and the supervisor.

5

Differentiating Performance-Based Supervision and Evaluation

You have now seen how a teacher and supervisor might embrace, understand, and launch the Performance-Based Supervision and Evaluation model under somewhat ideal circumstances. However, PBSE is effective with teachers at every point in their professional maturity and at every point in their ability to conceptualize how their instruction can affect student learning.

In Chapter 3, we introduced two of Marcia Williams' colleagues: 7th grade math teacher Eileen Blanchard (a "data-anemic" teacher) and physical education teacher Larry Rinaldi (a "data-prolific" teacher). In this chapter, we look at how Principal Gary Mulholland will need to differentiate his work with these two teachers as they get started on the PBSE pathway. Our intent is to illustrate the ways in which supervisors can adapt the process to the needs of all their staff members and ensure that they all acquire the professional development that they to support student learning.

Eileen's Story

◢ Eileen wasn't sure where to begin with Performance-Based Supervision and Evaluation. She thought this new approach seemed interesting, but she didn't know how to connect it to what she knew about grading or to her previous professional development plans.

After his first meeting with Eileen, Gary suspected she would need to take a slow and reiterative approach to the PBSE process. He used the Criteria of Excellence as a planning management tool to plot Eileen's present skill status and levels of understanding (see Figure 5.1). She had long administered 7th grade math quizzes and tests and recorded them faithfully in her grade book, and she followed the district curriculum for her 7th grade math lessons and units. But it seemed to Gary that Eileen knew little about math standards for 7th graders, whether at the district, state, or national level.

Figure 5.1
Eileen Blanchard's Teacher Preparation Phase Status—October

Indicator	Criteria
TP-1 __E__ **Start!** TP-2 __JB__	*The teacher has identified* • Student performance data that represent "essential learning" and are standards-based. • Student performance data that result from holistic assessment of a learning task requiring students to apply multiple skills and various knowledge.
TP-3 __JB__ TP-4 __JB__	*The teacher has organized* • Student performance data so that they may be viewed and interpreted in more than one way. • Student performance data to reveal student performance strengths and weaknesses.
TP-5 __JB__ TP-6 __JB__ TP-7 __JB__	*The teacher has completed an analysis of data, producing* • Some conclusions about student performance strengths and weaknesses. • Some artifacts of student work exemplifying student performance strengths and weaknesses. • Some ideas about how to modify teaching to bring about improved student learning in the areas targeted in the data analysis.

Evaluation Scale: C = Competent; E = Emergent; JB = Just Beginning

Gary and Eileen met briefly to discuss how she might get started. He explained that before their next meeting (their third overall), he wanted her to do some research into Web sites that identified state and national mathematics standards and find out what organizations like the National Council of Teachers of Mathematics (NCTM) considered "essential learning" for 7th graders. Eileen did, and she was amazed at what was available online: explicit expectations for students, clear delineations of both content knowledge and process skills, and related assessment measures. Eileen found that her investigations illuminated the district mathematics curriculum, forming a state and national context for what she taught in 7th grade. She came away from the investigation with a far better understanding about what her students should know and be able to do.

In their third meeting, Gary and Eileen discussed what she had learned about mathematics standards and her perceptions of her own students' understanding and knowledge relative to the standards. What stood out for Eileen was that her students typically fell short in their ability to conceptualize and use fractions, decimals, and percents in their mathematical computations and problem solving. It was a pattern she saw year after year.

As the meeting came to a close, Gary could see Eileen's increasing interest in her new learning, and he suggested that she gather some hard data about her students' performance. He pointed her in the direction of the state mastery test, which students at the middle school level took in both 6th and 8th grade. Eileen agreed to obtain and review a copy of last year's 6th grade scores (where she could find performance data for her current 7th graders). She would pay particular attention to student performance in the areas of suspected weakness—fractions, decimals, and percents—and she and Gary would discuss her findings when they met again in two weeks.

Connecting Essential Learning and Prompting Data. As Eileen learned more about the math standards articulated in her state mathematics framework, she developed a deeper appreciation for the essential knowledge and skills her students should be learning. However, she was less clear about how it connected to standardized testing or to her classroom instruction and assessments. After Eileen had obtained last year's schoolwide 6th grade scores from the guidance counselor, she found herself curious about how the test was organized relative to math standards and about the specific knowledge addressed in each standard. In particular, Eileen wondered if her perception was on the mark: were students in her school—or even statewide—*really* doing poorly in the area of fractions, decimals, and percents?

Seeking answers to these questions, Eileen spent more time exploring the state department of education Web site. There, she found a great deal of information about the state's mandated testing program, including blueprints for the latest "generation" of the assessment as well as a list of the standards it addressed and the specific "content strands," or subsets of skills, within each of those standards. This information began to make a bit more sense to Eileen because it seemed to represent more closely what she understood about mathematics curriculum and instruction.

Eileen soon realized that it might be easy to plot how Fairview students had performed in each standard and content strand area and then compare these data with the performance of 6th graders statewide over time. Another resource on the state department of education Web site offered quick access to this information. At this point, she was still not sure which content strands were connected to test items on fractions, decimals, and percents, so she decided to create a data table showing all the information, which would give her a broad picture of student performance (see Figure 5.2, p. 68).

The data table was revealing. Although Fairview Middle School was considered to be a high-performing school with an excellent curriculum and great extracurricular programs, the data suggested that students had begun to lose ground on the state mathematics test. And Eileen's suspicion had been right: the content strands addressing fractions, decimals, and percents were among the areas where performance had declined or remained noticeably low.

Eileen still wasn't absolutely sure about the specific content and skills represented in these standards and content strands. What exactly were these tests measuring? Were there topics that she (and perhaps her colleagues too?) either weren't teaching or weren't teaching to mastery level? Which were the items related to fractions, decimals, and percents?

As Eileen flipped through documents she had downloaded from state's Web site, she came across a potentially helpful resource: the report describing the blueprint for the "third generation" of the state test and indicating how items had changed since the last iteration (Connecticut State Department of Education, 2001a). Eileen compared the blueprint to the data table she had developed and marked those standards and content strands containing items related to fractions, decimals, and percents. It didn't take her long to realize that if she were to focus specifically on this area of learning, she did not need to be intensely concerned with all 25 content strands. Eileen modified her original table by eliminating content strands that were not related to fractions, decimals, and percents and expanding those that were (see Figure 5.3, p. 70).

As Eileen reviewed this more focused information about Fairview's performance, she was even more convinced that she needed to work with at least some of her students on fractions, decimals, and percents. When she next met with her principal, he recommended she consult one more resource to further clarify the essential learning represented on the state

Figure 5.2

A Comparison of School and Statewide 6th Grade Math Performance Data, 2002–2005

Content Standards and Content Strands*	School Data			Statewide Data		
	% Mastery 2002	% Mastery 2005	% Change	% Mastery 2002	% Mastery 2005	% Change
Number Sense						
1. Place Value	95	93	–2	91	92	+1
2. Pictorial Representation of Numbers	86	81	–5	80	78	–2
3. Equivalent Fractions, Decimals, Percents	77	69	–8	68	69	+1
4. Order, Magnitude, and Rounding of Numbers	89	86	–3	80	79	–1
Operations						
5. Models for Operations	75	74	–1	72	75	+3
6. Basic Facts	97	93	–4	92	88	–4
7. Computation with Whole Numbers and Decimals	87	83	–4	81	74	–7
8. Computation with Fractions	89	77	–12	82	75	–7
9. Solve Word Problems	97	93	–4	91	85	–6
Estimation and Approximation						
10. Numerical Estimation Strategies	97	93	–4	91	89	–2
11. Estimating Solutions to Problems	63	57	–6	45	44	–1
Measurement						
14. Time	81	86	+5	73	75	+2
15. Approximating Measures	85	72	–13	79	74	–5
16. Customary and Metric Measures	52	45	–7	45	46	+1
Spatial Relationships and Geometry						
17. Geometric Shapes and Properties	71	65	–6	74	65	–9
18. Spatial Relationships	99	97	–2	95	92	–3
Probability and Statistics						
19. Tables, Charts, and Graphs	95	95	—	91	93	+2

Figure 5.2 (*continued*)						
	School Data			**Statewide Data**		
Content Standards and Content Strands*	% Mastery 2002	% Mastery 2005	% Change	% Mastery 2002	% Mastery 2005	% Change
20. Statistics and Data Analysis	70	63	–7	62	56	–6
21. Probability	73	68	–5	69	61	–8
Patterns						
22. Patterns	85	88	+3	80	81	+1
Algebra and Functions						
23. Algebraic Concepts	89	95	+6	84	91	+7
Discrete Mathematics						
24. Classification and Logical Reasoning	85	89	+4	76	78	+2
Integrated Understandings						
25. Mathematical Understandings	27	26	–1	23	25	+2

*Content standards are indicated in bold; content strands are numbered.

Note: Content strands 12 and 13 are related to the standard on Ratios, Proportion, and Percent, which is not tested in 6th grade.

mathematics test: the handbook for the test's most recent version. Each math teacher had received a copy when the third generation was released a few years before, and at the time, the teachers had gotten together to look it over and become familiar with the sample items it described. It had been a while since Eileen had cracked the cover, but she thought that doing so now would help her complete a cycle of understanding about what her students needed to know and be able to do relative to fractions, decimals, and percents. In fact, Eileen realized that to plan instruction for her 7th graders, she really needed to consult the 8th grade content of the handbook: what did they need to learn this year to prepare them for next year?

Eileen knew that she would need support from Gary and other district resources to approach the next part of her work: developing a classroom assessment that would confirm that fractions, decimals, and percents were truly a worthy area of focus for a targeted group of students. Before she could identify a clear and strategic objective, she needed to take a step sideways and develop her own understanding of how to create, administer, and analyze standards-based classroom assessments.

Figure 5.3

A Comparison of School and Statewide 6th Grade Math Performance Data on Fractions, Decimals, and Percents, 2002–2005

Content Standards and Content Strands*	School Data			Statewide Data		
	% Mastery 2002	% Mastery 2005	% Change	% Mastery 2002	% Mastery 2005	% Change
Number Sense						
2. Pictorial Representation of Numbers	86	81	–5	80	78	–2
(2.a) Relate decimals (0.01–2.99) to pictorial representations and vice versa						
(2.b) Relate fractions and mixed numbers to pictures and vice versa						
(2.c) Construct pictorial representations of fractions, mixed numbers, and decimals						
3. Equivalent Fractions, Decimals, Percents	77	69	–8	68	69	+1
(3.a) Rename equivalent fractions						
(3.b) Rename equivalent mixed number and improper fractions						
4. Order, Magnitude, and Rounding of Numbers	89	86	–3	80	79	–1
(4.a) Order whole numbers less than 1,000						
(4.b) Order fractions, mixed numbers, and decimals						
(4.c) Describe the magnitude of whole numbers less than 100,000						
(4.d) Describe the magnitude of fractions, mixed numbers and decimals						
(4.e) Round whole numbers in a context						

Figure 5.3   *(continued)*

Content Standards and Content Strands*	School Data			Statewide Data		
	% Mastery 2002	% Mastery 2005	% Change	% Mastery 2002	% Mastery 2005	% Change
(4.f) Round decimals in a context						
(4.g) Locate points on number lines and scales						
Operations						
7. Computation with Whole Numbers and Decimals	87	83	−4	81	74	−7
(7.a) Add and subtract two-, three-, and four-digit whole numbers and money amounts less than $100						
(7.b) Multiply and divide multiples of 10 and 100 by 10 and 100						
(7.c) Multiply and divide two- and three-digit whole numbers and money amounts less than $10 by one-digit numbers						
8. Computation with Fractions	89	77	−12	82	75	−7
(8.a) Add and subtract fractions and mixed numbers with like denominators						

*Content standards are indicated in bold; content strands are numbered.

Note: Content strands 12 and 13 are related to the standard on Ratios, Proportion, and Percent, which is not tested in 6th grade.

Drafting a Professional Development Plan. Over the course of Eileen's work with Gary on the initiatives described, she developed a draft for a two-part professional development plan (see Figure 5.4, p. 72). It projected her own learning needs related to both collecting and analyzing data to improve student learning and developing classroom assessments to measure student progress. In Eileen's case, acquiring and making meaning of

Figure 5.4
A Model Professional Development Plan for the Data-Anemic Teacher

Plan for the Students	Time Line	Plan for the Teacher
	by October 3	• Initial meeting with supervisor to discuss PBSE.
	by October 15	• During October, meet with supervisor two or three times regarding collecting and analyzing prompting data. • Begin broad, Web-based investigation of math standards; in particular, investigate state standards related to fractions, decimals, and percents. • Begin to gather 6th grade math scores from the state assessment.
	by October 31	• Meet with supervisor to discuss mathematics standards, state scores, and hypotheses regarding potential focus for the professional development plan. ○ Investigate other local and statewide content experts and PD resources, activities, and readings related to math standards and the collection and analysis of student performance data.
	by November 15	• Sign up for the building inservice seminar on the collection and analysis of student performance data. • Begin PD readings related to collection and analysis of student performance data. • Meet with the district math department chairperson to learn about developing standards-based math units.
	by November 30	• Begin the building inservice seminar on data collection and analysis. • Determine specific standards-based knowledge and skills related to fractions, decimals, and percents (as seen through state assessment data and resources) and begin to analyze these data. • Draft a professional development plan.

	by December 1	• Develop a trial standards-based mathematics unit. • Develop a related standards-based rubric, also aligned with district curriculum, for assessing student knowledge and skills. • Meet with the district math department chairperson regarding standards-based math assessment.
• Teach the trial standards-based unit and use the related assessment.	by December 20	• Record notes on the implementation of the standards-based math unit and related assessment, as well as recommendations for improving future units.
	by January 15	• Develop a standards-based classroom performance assessment for fractions, decimals, and percents. • Develop a standards-based rubric for this assessment. • Continue the building inservice seminar on data collection and analysis.
• Administer a classroom performance assessment for fractions, decimals, and percents.	by January 20	• Update PD resources related to math standards; performance assessment for fractions, decimals, and percents; and data collection and analysis. • Continue the building inservice seminar on data collection and analysis.
	by January 31	• Analyze and review the classroom performance assessment for fractions, decimals, and percents. • Determine the target group for focused intervention. • Develop initial instructional interventions. • Meet with supervisor and district math department chairperson to review an analysis of the classroom performance assessment and the planned instructional interventions for targeted students.

○ Open bullets indicate activities reflective of more traditional models of supervision and evaluation.

(continued)

Figure 5.4 (continued)

Plan for the Students	Time Line	Plan for the Teacher
• Implement targeted instructional interventions in fractions, decimals, and percents.	by February 15	• Submit a mid-cycle report of progress on the professional development plan to supervisor, including evidence of teacher learning. ○ Schedule and complete the mid-cycle conference with the supervisor; modify professional development plan as needed. • Continue with the building inservice seminar on data collection and analysis.
• Continue to implement targeted instructional interventions, modifying them based on continuing analysis of student performance data.	by April 15	• Meet with the district math department chairperson regarding standards-based math instruction and assessment. • Develop a second performance assessment for fractions, decimals and percents. ○ Schedule and complete the supervisor's observation of intervention lessons, teacher–supervisor conferencing, and instructional adjustments.
• Administer a second performance assessment for fractions, decimals, and percents to the intervention group.	by May 1	○ Complete readings, consultations with math department chair and other experts, and any other PD activities. • Complete the building inservice seminar on data collection and analysis.
• Continue to implement targeted instructional interventions, modifying them as needed, based on student performance.	by May 5	• Complete an analysis and review of the second performance assessment data.
• Collect written reflection and comments from intervention group regarding their learning experiences.	by May 20	○ Submit results, including student comments, and a final report of progress to the supervisor. • Schedule and complete the summative conference and reflect on the year's professional development plan.

these *confirming* data would be part of her new learning. Her professional development plan also reflected her emerging concern about her students' learning needs in the area of fractions, decimals, and percents. ◢

Differentiating the Journey for Teachers Like Eileen

When reviewing Eileen's professional development plan, you may note, and perhaps question, that her direct instructional interventions to improve student learning do not begin until January, much later in the academic year than Marcia Williams began her interventions (see Figure 4.2). This is purposeful, and it raises an important issue.

In the PBSE model, all teachers walk the same pathway, but each does it at a needs-appropriate pace. As noted in Chapter 3, teachers who are just beginning to use student performance data strategically need a more measured start: time to develop sufficient conceptual understanding of the PBSE model and familiarity with what constitutes "essential learning," and time to investigate resources, which will allow them to drill deep into student performance data and set a meaningful, learning-based instructional target. We have found that this kind of extended investigation, based on individual initiative and the guidance of supervisors (i.e., a principal or a district-level content expert), increases teachers' engagement in the work. Their efforts begin to confirm and illuminate hypotheses about student learning needs, and the resonance is seductive. They not only become excited about their individual work, but find themselves also eager to participate in buildingwide inservice programs on topics like student performance data collection and analysis.

For teachers like Eileen, the shift from a more traditional conception of supervision and evaluation to one that is performance based requires continual coaching and support. To begin the process, Gary asks Eileen to become familiar with established standards for learning and to revisit her students' standardized test scores. As Eileen becomes more comfortable with and knowledgeable about Performance-Based Supervision and Evaluation, he will ask her to examine school and district priorities for student learning (the fourth of the "four tests"). The next step is to help Eileen see that holistic types of assessment offer an opportunity to encourage higher-order thinking in her students and to look more deeply at their work. This will involve a number of collaborative initiatives (with Gary himself and with an expert advisor), including coaching Eileen on various skill areas: the development of correlated, standards-based instructional units and classroom assessments; the use of a wide range of valid scoring rubrics that reflect both state standards and local curriculum mandates; and how to look at the data through several lenses to zero-in on an understanding of student learning needs.

Over a series of meetings, Gary's objective with Eileen is to make explicit the stages of awareness and understanding that Marcia Williams found more intuitive and natural in her own investigations.

◪ Gary was pleased with the professional development plan Eileen had drafted. As he had advised, the first half of the year was dedicated to teacher learning and did not include specific instructional interventions. It was possible that at the end of the school year, Eileen would still be at the "emerging" level of approach to PBSE. Still, in pursuing the initiatives in her plan, Eileen would learn a good deal about her mathematics standards, broaden her understanding of performance-based assessment, and develop at least two standards-based units of instruction and related assessments. She would even begin to collect and analyze action research data on student performance in ways that would be far more informative to instruction than recording scores in a grade book.

Significantly, while Eileen focused on her own learning, good things would be happening for her students. She would be implementing more holistic and more instructive assessments (Wiggins & McTighe, 1998), analyzing student performance in greater depth, and gaining a better idea of her students' learning and how to further it. Gary suspected that Eileen's professional development plan would be a two-year undertaking, but he knew that this slower pace would give her sufficient time to internalize the knowledge and skills necessary to use student performance data effectively. ◪

⛉ KEYSTONE

For a data-anemic teacher, the real professional growth during the preliminary stages of PBSE implementation is coming to understand that grades in and of themselves reveal little about student learning. The value of data comes from how well student performance represents essential learning and helps teachers to make informed, contextualized, and timely instructional decisions to address student learning needs.

Larry's Story

◪ To guide his differentiated supervisory work with physical education teacher Larry Rinaldi, Gary returned to the Teacher Preparation Phase of the Criteria of Excellence. His assessment of Larry's status is shown in Figure 5.5 (see p. 78).

Clearly, Larry was familiar with data collection and had aggregated a wealth of raw data. His next step was to learn how to organize the right data to inform his instructional practice. Gary asked Larry to put aside the piles of videotapes, progress reports, and classroom performance checklists, and to focus instead on the notion of "essential learning."

The physical education standards represented on the state fitness test provided an effective starting place. There were four test components that together focused on flexibility, strength, and endurance:

1. *A modified sit and reach* to measure flexibility of the lower back and hamstrings;

2. *Partial curl-ups* to measure abdominal strength and endurance;

3. *Right-angle push-ups* to measure upper-body strength and endurance; and

4. *A one-mile run/walk* to measure aerobic endurance.

Each of these tests was aligned with a state standard for fitness ("Students will use fitness concepts to achieve and maintain a health-enhancing level of physical fitness," Connecticut State Department of Education, 1998b). The standards also called for middle school physical education students to master the assessment's physiological indicators, apply principles of training to improve fitness, develop personal goals for a healthy lifestyle, participate in activities in and out of school, and achieve or make progress toward certain levels of mastery in areas related to the state fitness assessment.

Figure 5.5
Larry Rinaldi's Teacher Preparation Phase Status—October

Indicator	Criteria
TP-1 __C__ TP-2 __C__	*The teacher has identified* • Student performance data that represent "essential learning" and are standards-based. • Student performance data that result from holistic assessment of a learning task requiring students to apply multiple skills and various knowledge.
TP-3 __E__ **Start!** TP-4 __E__	*The teacher has organized* • Student performance data so that they may be viewed and interpreted in more than one way. • Student performance data to reveal student performance strengths and weaknesses.
TP-5 __E__ TP-6 __E__ TP-7 __JB__	*The teacher has completed an analysis of data, producing* • Some conclusions about student performance strengths and weaknesses. • Some artifacts of student work exemplifying student performance strengths and weaknesses. • Some ideas about how to modify teaching to bring about improved student learning in the areas targeted in the data analysis.

Evaluation Scale: C = Competent; E = Emergent; JB = Just Beginning

In the last few years, Gary had had a number of conversations with his PE teachers about Fairview students' performance on the state physical fitness test and classroom assessments. As a result, the principal already had a sense of what might be a logical area for Larry's improvement objective. Additionally, the state fitness assessment goals were also indicated in the Fairview PE curriculum and, based on the scores and on Larry's classroom assessments, these seemed to be areas of need. It was clear to Gary that flexibility, strength, and endurance represented an appropriate focus for Larry's interventions. ◢

Differentiating the Journey for Teachers Like Larry

Data-prolific teachers are almost always excited by the notion of using student performance data to inform instructional planning. The challenge when working with teachers like Larry is to help them find significant and relevant prompting data that are connected to essential learning, confirm areas of need through classroom assessments, and settle on a single, narrow improvement objective.

Gary's plan is to focus Larry on finding prompting data within all the standardized student performance records he already has on file. Once this has been accomplished, Gary and other district personnel with content-area expertise will need to guide Larry toward finding or developing classroom performance data to confirm that his intended area of focus was indeed significant. Finally, Larry will need to prioritize his focus on a "slice" of teaching and learning. He must identify both the exact physical education knowledge and skills he will track across the course of the academic year and the students for whom he will plan interventions.

◢ Gary welcomed Larry to his office after school and began their conversation by focusing on the state fitness test. As requested, Larry brought all his information on Fairview student performance over the last few years. He had saved several years' worth of the composite score sheets and was familiar with the four components of the test. Gary suggested that, together, they develop a way to organize student performance data from each of the four fitness tests to see how the Fairview students had done over time. Larry remarked that he was curious about how his students matched up against their peers throughout the state. He also noted that, in his experience, girls did not achieve as high a level of fitness as boys, and that he often worried that the current physical education program did not sufficiently promote stronger progress by female students.

Together, Larry and his principal organized and recorded their aggregated data into a table (see Figure 5.6, p. 80). Although Larry had previously prepared an annual summary of his students' fitness scores, this was the first time he had seen the data organized in ways that allowed comparison and suggested trends over time.

For both educators, a few facts were clear right from the start: boys generally outperformed girls on all four tests; girls performed least well on right-angle push-ups; and although Fairview students performed above

Figure 5.6
Performance Data from the State Physical Fitness Assessment

1. School Data: Percent Passing the State Assessments by Grade and Gender, 2001–2005

Test	Year	Grade 6 (% Passing)			Grade 8 (% Passing)		
		Boys	Girls	All	Boys	Girls	All
Modified Sit	01–02	66	58	62.4	67	60	64.2
and Reach	02–03	52	49	50.7	53	51	51.1
	03–04	55	52	53.7	55	52	53.7
	04–05	59	53	56.2	54	46	50.2
Partial	01–02	62	56	59.4	64	59	62.6
Curl-Ups	02–03	58	46	52.5	60	47	53.8
	03–04	60	51	56.3	62	54	59.0
	04–05	57	52	55.1	54	43	49.3
Right-Angle	01–02	57	36	48.8	59	38	49.8
Push-Ups	02–03	52	37	45.4	48	32	41.4
	03–04	56	37	47.3	56	37	47.6
	04–05	58	37	48.5	55	35	45.4
One-Mile	01–02	58	46	52.3	58	52	55.4
Run/Walk	02–03	52	42	47.2	45	42	43.2
	03–04	55	40	48.4	52	46	49.4
	04–05	56	45	51.6	47	41	44.3

2. School and State Data Comparison: Percent Passing All Four Tests by Grade and Gender, 2001–2005

Year	School Grade 6 (% Passing)			State Grade 6 (% Passing)	School Grade 8 (% Passing)			State Grade 8 (% Passing)
	Boys	Girls	All	All	Boys	Girls	All	All
01–02	57.2	35.2	46.2	38.4	56.7	37.3	47.0	40.6
02–03	51.2	37.0	44.1	33.3	44.8	31.6	38.2	35.5
03–04	54.9	36.5	45.7	33.7	51.4	36.4	43.9	35.5
04–05	55.1	36.7	45.9	33.8	45.9	34.5	40.2	35.3

state averages, there was still much to be done to improve their strength, flexibility, and endurance.

Because of his pride in his students and in the Fairview physical education program, Larry was understandably disappointed at the less than stellar picture that emerged from the data. But, he commented to Gary, it was somewhat gratifying to see that his perceptions about girls' performance were well founded. He also saw how the data could help him make decisions about additional information he might need and give him ideas about how he might obtain it.

When Gary and Larry connected for their third meeting, Larry's enthusiasm for working within a PBSE model was heightened. He was excited about using student performance data to plan more specific instruction and eager to share the idea he had: he would gather individual state fitness assessment data for all of last year's 6th graders, focus on the lowest area of performance, and then develop instructional interventions to be implemented in all 7th grade classes in the academic year ahead.

Gary raised a cautionary point. It was unlikely that all the 7th grade students—approximately 200 boys and girls—would need the intervention suggested by the average performance scores. Further, individual performance data might suggest that some students would need significant intervention in certain areas. For Larry to understand his students' specific learning needs, he would need to disaggregate his data further and look at it through several lenses.

Gary suggested the following course of action:

1. Focus on program trends by comparing the performance of the same cohort of students in 6th grade and 8th grade. (For example, Larry might compare the 6th grade scores from the 2000–2001 school year with the 8th grade scores from the 2002–2003 school year.)

2. Specifically investigate the essential learning associated with each of the four tests by exploring the connection between the test and state content standards, as well as how these skills related to Fairview's physical education curriculum units.

3. Identify local or "internal" resources (perhaps the district physical education chairperson or a PE teacher who has served on a curriculum committee) willing to help Larry align his instructional units and lessons with physical education standards, develop standards-based classroom assessments to obtain confirming data, and zero-in on the target group for instructional interventions.

4. Identify potential "external" professional development resources, such as university, state, or national contacts, projects, organizations, and Web sites.

5. Look more closely at the individual performance of the students with the lowest scores.

6. Draft an improvement objective to serve as the foundation of his professional development plan.

As their meeting came to a close, Gary encouraged Larry to begin thinking about the PBSE model and its intentional focus on "getting smarter" about instruction and assessment related to a specific slice of essential learning. Gary warned the PE teacher that this might very well mean working more intensely with a small group of students, rather than an entire class section or a full grade level. Because Larry's understanding of the work had progressed so well, Gary also encouraged him to begin drafting the professional development plan that would support his efforts to narrow and focus his work with student performance data. Two weeks later, Larry presented his principal with a draft plan (see Figure 5.7).

After reviewing Larry's professional development plan and thinking about their last meeting, Gary was optimistic that the PE teacher was well on his way to developing strategic instructional interventions for students needing support in specific physical education skills and competencies. He knew it had been difficult for Larry, accustomed to collecting lots of data from lots of students, to conceive of an instructional intervention involving only 15 or so students. Gary also knew that part of his ongoing role would be to help Larry see how knowledge acquired to improve the fitness of this small group of students would influence the instruction he provided for all his students. Finally, Gary noted with pleasure that although this style of data analysis, intervention, and assessment was new for Larry, the PE teacher was quickly becoming more comfortable and competent with the process. Gary anticipated that without much more coaching, Larry would easily become a solid resource for colleagues still needing support with PBSE. ◪

—————————— ▽ KEYSTONE ——————————

For the "data-prolific" teacher, collecting extensive student performance data need not be the way to truly understand student learning or demonstrate extraordinary professional dedication. Giving a teacher "permission" to work with a small group of students on an instructional intervention is both revolutionary and an opportunity to improve instructional effectiveness in areas of essential learning. The depth of instructional understanding the teacher acquires by working with a select cohort of students to improve specific skills can later be applied to broader groups of students.

Figure 5.7
A Model Professional Development Plan for the Data-Prolific Teacher

Plan for the Students	Time Line	Plan for the Teacher
	by October 3	• Initial meeting with supervisor to discuss PBSE.
	by October 10	• Begin to collect and examine student performance data on the state fitness assessment for the last four years. • Begin to gather focused PD resources related to essential learning in PE and to the collection and analysis of student performance data for instructional planning.
	by October 20	• Meet regularly with supervisor to discuss student fitness performance data. • Begin PD readings related to the collection and analysis of student fitness performance data.
	by November 1	• Begin to disaggregate the 6th grade state fitness assessment scores for each of the four subtests and among groups of students. • Meet with the district PE department chairperson regarding standards-based instruction and assessment. • Draft a professional development plan.
	by November 10	• Sign up for the building inservice seminar on the collection and analysis of student performance data. ○ Investigate confirming data from existing classroom assessments. If this is unavailable, draft a new classroom assessment related to the state fitness assessment.

○ Open bullets indicate activities reflective of more traditional models of supervision and evaluation.

(continued)

Figure 5.7 (*continued*)

Plan for the Students	Time Line	Plan for the Teacher
• Administer the standards-based assessment to students in 7th grade PE classes.	by November 20	• Develop a standards-based rubric that is aligned with district curriculum for assessing fitness in the target skill areas.
	by November 30	• Begin the building inservice seminar on data collection and analysis. • Using the standards-based rubric, evaluate student performance on the assessment and analyze performance data from the standards-based assessment. • Determine the cohort of students who will receive instructional interventions during "open gym" period or after school; this will be a small group (15 or so students). • Determine the specific knowledge and skills related to the targeted fitness needs.
	by December 10	• Investigate internal and external PD resources in the teaching and assessment of the specific knowledge and skills related to the targeted fitness needs. • Continue to participate in the building inservice seminar on data collection and analysis.
	by January 15	○ Participate in PD activities for the teaching and assessment of the specific knowledge and skills related to the targeted fitness needs. • Draft focused interventions for the target group of students.

by January 30	• Involve the target cohort of students in additional fitness interventions during the "open gym" period or after school. • Embed the assessed skills into all 7th grade PE classes through integration into existing units of instruction.	• Investigate statewide professional development activities, content experts, and professional readings related to the assessed fitness skills. • Continue to meet with the district PE department chairperson and other content experts regarding standards-based instruction and assessment.
by February 10	• Continue instructional interventions in the target fitness areas, modifying interventions based on continuing analysis of student performance data.	• Submit a mid-cycle report of progress in student learning. ○ Schedule and complete the mid-cycle conference with supervisor; modify the professional development plan as needed. • Continue to participate in the building inservice seminar on data collection and analysis.
by April 15		○ Schedule and complete supervisor's observation of intervention lessons (in class and through additional instructional time), teacher–supervisor conferencing, and instructional adjustments. • Continue to meet with the district PE department chairperson and other content experts regarding standards-based instruction and assessment. • Develop a second assessment to monitor the progress of the target group.
by May 1	• Administer a second assessment of targeted fitness areas to the target group.	• Complete the building inservice seminar on data collection and analysis. ○ Complete readings, consultations with fitness experts, and other PD activities.
by May 5		• Complete the analysis and review of the second fitness assessment data, using the same standards-based rubric.
by May 20		○ Submit results and the final report of progress to supervisor. ○ Schedule and complete summary conference and reflect on the year's professional development plan.

A Few Last Thoughts About Differentiating PBSE

Performance-Based Supervision and Evaluation opens new opportunities for both teacher and student learning. Because PBSE asks teachers to invest energy in analyzing a slice of student performance, they are led to think deeply about student learning and the ways in which they might address specific learning needs.

The PBSE process can easily be individualized for all teachers and staff members, using the Criteria of Excellence continuum as a framework for developing individual professional development plans. Further, as supervisors come to a better understanding of their staff members' specific development needs, they can make adjustments throughout all six phases of the PBSE model for both individual teachers and groups of teachers with common learning goals. Some teachers may need to revise their improvement objective slightly or adjust the timing of certain activities within their professional development plans; others, like Eileen Blanchard, may need to pause to acquire more foundational knowledge and skills before proceeding with their original plans. It is important to note that these modifications are prompted by the teacher's learning needs, not by a calendar that requires tasks to be completed by certain dates. Teachers' individual pathways may vary, but one thing is certain: by coming to understand the intent and process of the PBSE model, they will significantly increase their capacity to support student learning, especially for children who have specific learning needs.

6

Managing
Performance-Based
Supervision and Evaluation

◪ Principal Gary Mulholland leaned back in his office chair for a few moments of reflection. He had just completed his first round of conferences with Fairview faculty, and, as he had expected, the majority of his teachers were able to identify and analyze areas of essential learning where support was required. A few had even determined a cohort of students who would need targeted intervention.

Still, there were some teachers who would need continuing coaching to help them drill deep into data, plan effective professional development, and determine the most appropriate instructional interventions for their students. There were also a handful of faculty members who were already grumbling about PBSE as "one more thing" on their already full professional plates. And then there was the important matter of professional development. How would Gary muster the resources—people, materials, time, and budget—to meet the teachers' individual and collective needs? Gary knew he had his work cut out for him. ◪

There is no question about it: Performance-Based Supervision and Evaluation is *not* business as usual. Administrators implementing this model will find that managing teacher supervision demands a different kind of planning and a much different approach to distributing resources. It is, in essence, a cultural shift in supervisory thinking and action in regard to buildingwide professional development, individualized professional development, supervision, accountability, and dealing with resistance. While supervisors will need to be organized to implement PBSE effectively, most will find that the work is, to some extent, front-loaded. Teachers typically approach their roles in this process very professionally, and once the model is up and running, it usually proceeds smoothly. Furthermore, the shift to PBSE offers administrators the opportunity to use resources in ways that genuinely improve student learning, rather than perpetuating past practice just because "we've always done it that way."

Professional Development Planning: Grounded in Data

The professional development familiar to most teachers and administrators is planned months in advance. Sometimes this reflects the logistical need to book guest speakers and facilities early. Sometimes it's because district norms prescribe a calendar for professional development planning to coordinate events and participants. And sometimes it's because implementing new programs or instructional methods demands concurrent staff development. Generally speaking, the standard "six months ahead" approach is associated with predicted professional development needs—most notably those representing the "outside in" initiatives of the day.

If "outside in" professional development planning is the norm, PBSE professional development planning is "inside out." Within this model, principals like Gary Mulholland make decisions about which professional development initiatives to pursue and fund based on teachers' emerging needs, especially regarding their capacity to use student performance data to inform practice. This is a much different approach than externally predetermined professional development, and it requires new ways of thinking about the instructional growth of our faculties.

Planning professional development in the PBSE model rests on a number of assumptions:

• Each administrator and school must agree on a threshold for determining group versus individual budgeting for professional development. In our work with schools and districts, we advise that expenditures for group professional development strategies are justified when 25 percent or more of the faculty present common professional development needs.

• Group professional development must contribute to the professional development plan for the entire school.

• Professional development plans for individual teachers and groups of teachers evolve as the PBSE process unfolds. Individual professional development plans may change throughout the year as the teacher's learning needs change. Typically, group staff development is determined both by the collective teacher need status at the close of one school year and by what these teachers discover at the start of the next school year when they address their newly developed student learning objectives. Although we have shown Principal Gary Mulholland begin a new school year by working with his staff to uncover their professional development needs, once PBSE is fully implemented within a school, these assessments begin in the second semester of the school year, ideally during end-of-year conferences between teachers and administrators.

• To support each faculty member's new learning, a substantial portion of the professional development budget—as much as 75 percent—should be conserved for individual needs. As the PBSE process unfolds, the supervisor and teacher must be free to make contextualized professional development choices that are relevant to each teacher's journey as a learner. These choices are impossible to predict six months ahead of time.

• School-based decisions about group and individual professional development needs may or may not connect to district inservice initiatives. From the standpoint of determining strategic professional development, it makes sense for a school to connect to district initiatives when these relate to the common needs of the school's faculty. A number of approaches to instruction—differentiated instruction, multiple intelligence strategies, and concept-based curriculum, for example—certainly have merit and are effective in supporting student learning. However, when the prioritized needs of the faculty diverge from a district's initiative, the school must be free to pursue the course most pertinent to improving *its* students' learning.

─────────────── ▽ KEYSTONE ───────────────

In the PBSE model, planning and budgeting are *strategic, dynamic,* and *responsive* to the individual and collective needs of adult learners in order to provide the most effective support for student learners.

Planning Group Professional Development

In Performance-Based Supervision and Evaluation, administrators plan for building-level professional development activities in a manner that parallels the work teachers are doing: they gather data, view them in several ways, and use them to inform decision making. A look at Gary Mulholland's initiatives at Fairview Middle School will shed light on the process.

◢ Mindful of the importance of making decisions grounded in data, Gary turned to the Criteria of Excellence for help in synthesizing what he had learned in his round of faculty conferences. He gathered the individual Criteria of Excellence planning sheets he had completed after the initial conferences and set out to get an overview of his teachers' current status on the PBSE indicators. Because most had demonstrated a variety of skill levels within the Teacher Preparation Phase, he began with this stage of the continuum, noting the aggregate number and percent of teachers whose skills he had determined to be competent, emergent, or just beginning. Gary's summary for the 46 Fairview Middle School teachers is shown in Figure 6.1.

The Criteria of Excellence planning sheet was useful for recording initial data, but Gary found it a bit difficult to see patterns among teacher skills on the indicators. He decided to reorganize the information by creating a quick spreadsheet showing the percentage of teachers at each skill level, and then, being a visual person, also translated the spreadsheet into a bar chart (see Figure 6.2, p. 92). This gave him both an overall view of staff strengths for each indicator and a representation of where there was room for improvement.

Figure 6.1
Teacher Preparation Phase: Summary of Teachers' Skill-Level
Status—October

Indicator	Criteria
	The teacher has identified
TP-1 ✓	• Student performance data that represent "essential learning" and are standards-based. **Competent: 32 (69%); Emerging: 9 (20%); Just Beginning: 5 (11%)**
TP-2 ✓	• Student performance data that result from holistic assessment of a learning task requiring students to apply multiple skills and various knowledge. **Competent: 10 (22%); Emerging: 28 (61%); Just Beginning: 8 (17%)**
	The teacher has organized
TP-3 ✓	• Student performance data so that they may be viewed and interpreted in more than one way. **Competent: 9 (20%); Emergent: 22 (48%); Just Beginning: 15 (32%)**
TP-4 ✓	• Student performance data to reveal student performance strengths and weaknesses. **Competent: 29 (63%); Emergent: 12 (26%); Just Beginning: 5 (11%)**
	The teacher has completed an analysis of data, producing
TP-5 ✓	• Some conclusions about student performance strengths and weaknesses. **Competent: 22 (48%); Emergent: 18 (39%); Just Beginning: 6 (13%)**
TP-6 ✓	• Some artifacts of student work exemplifying student performance strengths and weaknesses. **Competent: 18 (39%); Emergent: 20 (44%); Just Beginning: 8 (17%)**
TP-7 ✓	• Some ideas about how to modify teaching to bring about improved student learning in the areas targeted in the data analysis. **Competent: 21 (45%); Emergent: 16 (35%); Just Beginning: 9 (20%)**
Evaluation Scale: C = Competent; E = Emergent; JB = Just Beginning	

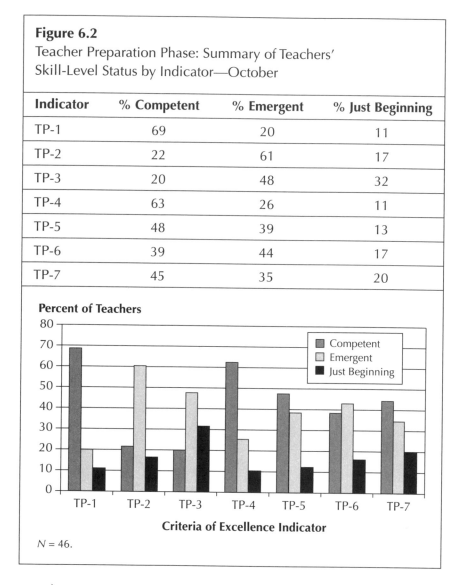

Figure 6.2
Teacher Preparation Phase: Summary of Teachers'
Skill-Level Status by Indicator—October

Indicator	% Competent	% Emergent	% Just Beginning
TP-1	69	20	11
TP-2	22	61	17
TP-3	20	48	32
TP-4	63	26	11
TP-5	48	39	13
TP-6	39	44	17
TP-7	45	35	20

Percent of Teachers

Criteria of Excellence Indicator

$N = 46$.

The picture was now clearer: Many teachers were able to identify what qualified as standards-based, essential learning (TP-1) and able to show their students' performance in a way that communicated areas of strength and weakness (TP-4). However, Gary recalled that several of these analyses had been a fairly basic portrayal of standardized test scores. Most teachers had a reasonable amount of information but seemed unsure about what to do with it.

The spreadsheet and graph clearly conveyed skill areas where teachers might need professional development support. Gary clustered the areas into two groups. The first he labeled "Proficiency in Deep Analysis of Student Data." This encompassed the general need to learn more about organizing data in different ways (TP-3), drawing meaningful and detailed conclusions from data (TP-5), incorporating a review of artifacts of student work into data analysis (TP-6), and developing the most relevant instructional interventions in response to data findings (TP-7). Gary labeled the second area of need "Proficiency in Creating Performance-Based and Holistic Assessments," which related to getting a picture of how students apply knowledge in the classroom (TP-2).

The next step for Gary was to develop sustained buildingwide inservice opportunities in these areas. He would allocate 25 percent of his professional development budget to this purpose. Ultimately, he set up a series of staff development seminars on each of the two topics, drawing facilitators from school and district experts and acquiring resources from a regional educational service center. The sessions for both seminars would be conducted during district professional development days, at established faculty meeting times, and during after-school meetings. ◢

Gary's example illustrates how, within the PBSE model, gathering data, viewing that data in several ways, and using them to inform decision making is as important for supervisors as it is for teachers. The benefits are many:

• The supervisor personally experiences the process and models it for teachers, lending credibility and alignment to the professional culture of the school.

• Decisions are grounded in data that are examined in depth.

• Planning based on these decisions is directly relevant to faculty needs and, therefore, strategic.

• Expenditures for professional development are aligned with both school and district priorities and, therefore, justifiable when resources are limited.

Planning Individual Professional Development

Some administrators may find this aspect of Performance-Based Supervision and Evaluation a bit daunting, as each teacher's individual development needs emerge from the teacher's work to isolate the slice of student learning that will be the focus of instructional interventions throughout the year. The teacher and supervisor mutually decide what new learning the teacher needs to "get smarter" in the target area. For some, it is additional content knowledge; for others, it is new pedagogical skills. The supervisor's role is to help the teacher connect with internal and external professional development resources that will best help that teacher learn how to address the targeted focus more effectively.

The collaborative crafting of an individual professional development plan begins with both the teacher and supervisor investigating potential resources for the teacher's new learning. These certainly include traditional professional development options, such as conferences and workshops; professional publications, including articles, books, and videos; and coursework at a nearby college or university. However, we would argue that some of the most effective professional development is derived through sustained, formal or informal direct interaction with a person who has expertise relevant to the target area. Here are some suggestions for identifying such experts, connecting to them for professional development, and building a continuum of resources.

• *Begin with the school's internal resources.* There is a wealth of knowledge and expertise among faculty and administrators within every school. Seek out teachers and teacher leaders who are known to be strong in a specific area of curriculum, instruction, or assessment, especially those who hold comparable professional positions. Also seek out in-school support personnel, like reading resource teachers. Working with a colleague tends to be less intimidating than working with an "outside" expert, and the proximity encourages that the connection will be maintained. And don't forget about peer coaching. Partnering two teachers whose improvement objectives focus on similar teaching or learning encourages mutually supportive collaboration and can lead to growth beyond what each might have accomplished alone.

• *Explore the district's internal resources.* There are likely to be specialist staff, department chairpersons, and district coordinators who can offer advice and support. Some districts, particularly larger ones, have positions fully dedicated to curriculum, instruction, and assessment support.

- *Contact regional educational service centers.* These are a great source for information on workshops, speakers, and consultation services.
- *Develop a partnership with area colleges and universities.* Higher education partners offer a research-based filter for evaluation of professional practice, professional development for faculty and administration, and an objective set of eyes during the supervision and evaluation process. Conversely, these partnerships also give universities the opportunity to connect theory with practice in an applied setting.
- *Join a national network of educators seeking to improve professional practice.* Seeking out consortia, participating in conferences, joining electronic forums, and subscribing to newsletters all broaden educators' opportunities to obtain updated information, discuss common experiences, and get suggestions for dealing with new issues.

A quick review of the professional development plans of the Fairview teachers (see Chapters 4 and 5) illustrates how various school and district personnel can support teacher development:

- Marcia Williams, the 8th grade social studies teacher, has committed to informal coaching on writing instruction and assessment provided by the school writing expert.
- Eileen Blanchard, the 7th grade mathematics teacher, has committed to working with the district math department chairperson to learn more about developing standards-based math units and assessments.
- Physical education teacher Larry Rinaldi has committed to working with the district's physical education department chairperson to obtain support in standards-based instruction and assessment in physical education.

Our emphasis on seeking support from school and district personnel resources—expert colleagues, reading consultants, math coordinators, curriculum specialists, and the like—derives from more than pragmatic considerations. We genuinely believe that these individuals' knowledge and skills are too often underutilized. Specialists and support staff who provide services to students on a "pullout" basis (or to the side or back of the classroom) can find it difficult to share their expertise with classroom teachers. The PBSE model encourages real collaboration and sharing: the classroom teacher develops the "need to know" motivation to learn from the specialist, and the specialist has an opportunity to provide expert guidance and instructional leadership.

────────────────── ▽ KEYSTONE ──────────────────

An important outcome of PBSE professional development is its redefinition of the responsibilities of, roles of, and relationships among teachers, specialized support staff, and administrators. Empowering these individuals to build personal capacity for teaching, learning, and leading increases overall instructional capacity throughout the school.

Supervisory Processes: Strategically Focused

A principal's typical supervision responsibilities include meetings to plan and monitor teacher professional development initiatives, regularly scheduled classroom observations, and end-of-year summative evaluations of faculty performance. And, yes, most districts prescribe an array of forms and templates to be certain that teachers and administrators "complete the paperwork" associated with each of these activities.

Administrators can and do integrate the PBSE model with preexisting district supervision and evaluation plans. What is unique about PBSE is how principals and teachers use the components of traditional supervision:

- In PBSE, initial meetings to establish a professional development plan focus on identifying a slice of essential learning through analysis of student performance data.
- The professional development plan organizes the teacher's new learning around what he or she requires to address student needs relative to the identified slice of essential learning.
- The mid-year review conference is an opportunity to discuss and demonstrate the teacher's progress with the professional development plan and to make any adjustments that are needed for the second half of the year.
- Classroom observations focus on the student learning objective and are timed to support teacher learning.
- The summative review conference offers the teacher the opportunity to provide evidence that professional development activities have directly and positively affected student learning.

The role of classroom observations within the PBSE model merits a bit of further discussion. As noted, the teacher and supervisor schedule classroom observations to take place at times when the teacher is applying skills acquired as part of the development plan. As a result, classroom observations are *purposeful,* that is, conducted so that that supervisor may provide timely feedback on the teacher's learning and suggest relevant follow-up activities. In the process, the teacher's growth is contextualized, continuous, and authentic (Glickman, Gordon, & Ross-Gordon, 2004).

The most powerful aspect of a PBSE classroom observation can be what follows it: the post-observation conversation between the teacher and administrator. We recommend scheduling the post-observation conference to take place *after* the teacher has administered a classroom performance assessment related to the lesson observed. This allows the teacher and supervisor to discuss real student work and conduct real analysis of student performance in real time.

Here are some sample questions that a supervisor might use to guide a post-observation conversation:

• What essential knowledge and skills are the focus of your unit and of this lesson in particular?

• How does your performance assessment evaluate these essential knowledge and skills? What specific indicators of learning formed the basis of your assessment?

• How have you analyzed the performance of your class, both collectively and individually? What does this analysis show?

• What does your analysis of student performance suggest regarding modification of curriculum, instruction, and assessment—for the whole class and for individual students?

During a post-observation conference, the teacher and supervisor should also discuss the teacher's new learning and the progress being made in applying that learning in the classroom. In our experience, teachers typically report that they feel better prepared to meet student needs and that they are impressed with the amount of rich information their data analyses offer. Looking at student data from a variety of perspectives allows them to observe patterns of performance for the entire class and across individual students. The analysis may also uncover areas of knowledge and skills that the teacher needs to learn more about. If so, the teacher and supervisor should map out ideas to pursue that learning through further professional development.

───────────────── ▽ KEYSTONE ─────────────────

Through supervisory efforts that are aligned with students' learning needs and the teacher's professional development experiences, every teacher develops greater instructional capacity, which can then be generalized to similar pedagogical needs. As a result, PBSE challenges the notion of the "marginal teacher," for every teacher can be empowered, regardless of where they begin in their PBSE orientation.

Accountability: Documenting Teachers' Growth

Supervisors and teachers first learning about PBSE often have questions about how faculty members can demonstrate that they have fulfilled their professional obligations, particularly in regard to established district evaluation plans. Clearly, required paperwork for any pre-existing evaluation plan can and should be completed, albeit in a way that refocuses the content of notes and reports on the teacher's efforts to grow professionally in response to specific, identified student learning needs.

Artifacts associated with specific initiatives in a professional development plan provide another mechanism for demonstrating accountability by documenting the teacher's progress toward increased instructional capacity. Here are just some of the artifacts that might be used in this manner:

• The teacher's initial memo to the supervisor reporting the analysis of student performance in an area of essential learning. Reports of student performance in the target area will be equally important for the mid-cycle review conference and the summative review conference.

• A list or database of resources on state and national curriculum standards in the target content area, as well as copies of this material.

• Memos summarizing what the teacher learned from investigating potential professional development resources related to the target area.

• Written synopses of reference materials read.

• A summary of new learning acquired at a conference or workshop.

• Materials developed as a result of building-level inservice seminars.

• Written reflections on new learning obtained through interactions with colleagues or external experts.

• Reflective notes on the effectiveness of interventions in the target area.

• Lessons or units of instruction developed as a result of new teacher learning.

• Holistic or performance-based assessments, including rubrics, developed as a result of new teacher learning.

• Student responses to these assessments, as well as other examples of student work.

• Student comments.

Although not an exhaustive list, these potential artifacts offer a wide array of possible vehicles for making the teacher's professional development efforts and new learning explicit. More importantly, when used as a point of conversation with colleagues and administrators, they generate rich discussion around authentic and strategic teacher and student learning. Appendix B offers concrete representations of what some of these artifacts might look like for our mathematics teacher, Eileen Blanchard.

Dealing with Resistance, Leading for Change

Wherever there is change, there will be those who have a difficult time adjusting to it and accepting new ways. In our work with teachers and administrators who are implementing PBSE, we have found this to be the case.

◢ During the last week of October, the biweekly Team Leaders' meeting in Gary Mulholland's office was nearing an end, and the last item on the agenda was the "Open Forum," an opportunity for any team leader to introduce a new item for discussion. There was a low cough from Larry Rinaldi, the team leader for the specialist staff.

"Well, Gary," he said, "we wanted you to know that there has been some grumbling among the troops about the Performance-Based Supervision and Evaluation program. Some of the staff members have been complaining to us that they already feel overworked, and that this is just one more new thing that we'll do for a couple of years and then move on to the next 'silver bullet.' A few people are not happy about the extra work."

Laura Soares, the team leader for 6th grade, chimed in. "Yes, and I'm hearing some complaining about the data-analysis part. A couple of my colleagues feel it's just overkill. They're not psychometricians! They feel their job is to *teach,* not to crunch numbers."

Gary took a moment to shape his reply. "Any time we change the way things are done, some folks will be uncomfortable with it or even negative about it. We need to give this program a fair try, because it has the power to significantly improve student learning. It will take time and a genuine effort by every one of us to use this process to help our students learn. Perhaps it's impossible for me to convince every teacher that this is the 'real deal.' But ultimately, when everyone starts experiencing for themselves the impact that their work is having on students, I think they'll recognize the rewards of their efforts." ◣

The administrator's role in leading for change is a complex one, requiring him or her to inform, facilitate, cheerlead, support, empower, and, if necessary, confront. Fortunately, a basic assumption remains true, even with teachers reluctant about change: educators want their students to learn, to learn what they should be learning, and to learn it at challenging levels. Most of us realize that dedication and hard work do not always yield the student performance we hope for. In order to achieve breakthroughs for students who find it hardest to learn—those with specific and identifiable learning needs—our intervention must be focused and strategic. This is the revelation most often experienced by teachers using Performance-Based Supervision and Evaluation.

Based on our experiences with the model's implementation, we suggest administrators try the following strategies to support a positive change process:

• Begin with encouragement and support.

• Be sure that everyone has a clear understanding of the model and their responsibilities within it.

• Secure the necessary resources to support faculty members and be sure these resources are in place when they are needed.

• Dedicate the lion's share of your energy to the majority of the faculty in order to support them as the school culture changes.

• Celebrate successes often and publicly. During the early stages of adopting the PBSE model, there will be teachers whose work yields positive outcomes fairly quickly, either in terms of their own instructional growth or in their students' performance. Acknowledging these successes at a faculty meeting or other public gathering can be both reinforcing and encouraging. Continue to publicize the positive efforts of faculty members throughout the year. Consider holding an end-of-year celebration featuring displays of teacher work related to their student learning objectives. This is a way to recognize teachers' efforts and encourage them to share what they have learned with colleagues.

• Offer close collaboration to those who are more resistant.

We want to offer a few additional words about resistant teachers. These individuals are not always outspoken in their opposition, but within the PBSE model, they identify themselves soon enough by their lack of participation in the process. If facilitation and support are not effective in engaging them in PBSE, a more assertive path is called for: one that incorporates checking in regularly to make sure tasks are completed, however reluctantly. It is particularly advisable to do this when these teachers are (or should be) undertaking data disaggregation during the Teacher Preparation Phase. This step is often an eye-opening one for resistant teachers, because in the process of doing it, many find themselves learning new skills for examining student performance. The benefits of the work are obvious and immediate.

In our experience, as the PBSE process continues and the positive impact on student learning becomes more and more evident, the attitudes of resistant teachers gradually change. Those who are able to change their pedagogy from a behavioral standpoint find that the positive effects of this change eventually modify their perceptions and attitudes and help them to feel more positive about the change in general (DuFour & Eaker, 1998).

A Few Final Notes About the Role of the Supervisor

Principal Gary Mulholland and the many administrators and supervisors he represents may legitimately wonder whether he will be able to put the components of the PBSE model in place for all his faculty members. It is a challenging task, but the answer is definitely yes, provided that the supervisor begins to work with faculty members wherever they are on the continuum of the Criteria of Excellence. It's vital that teachers move along that continuum at a pace that permits them to deepen their own learning, but they should be encouraged to apply that new learning to their instructional interventions as soon as professionally feasible. The model also makes the supervisor's work very interesting, because faculty members will be at different places in their development and will be pursuing relevant, authentic, and individualized professional development plans. Further, the model enables the supervisor to plan and enact meaningful collective professional development based on the common needs of the faculty as a whole.

Finally, because the focus of the student learning objective must align with the priorities of the school and district (remember the "four tests"?), the work of each teacher and supervisor coordinates with school and district improvement efforts. By design, alignment flows from the classroom, to the school, to the entire district, contributing to the collective capacity to support student learning.

─────────────── ▽ KEYSTONE ───────────────

PBSE also "re-professionalizes" the work of the supervisor. Teacher–supervisor discussions center on real student work, relevant teacher learning, and continuous capacity building.

7

Pursuing
Teacher Learning to Inform
Instructional Interventions

All that we have discussed to this point sets the stage for teacher learning, instructional interventions, ongoing assessment of student performance, and the supervisory activities that support Performance-Based Supervision and Evaluation and underscore its "systems thinking" (Senge, 1990) approach. With PBSE, teachers are responsible for taking charge of their own professional growth and translating it into instructional interventions that lead to better learning. While the supervisor fosters professional development connections, monitors progress, and ultimately makes judgments and recommendations, the teachers have substantial autonomy and lead the way, based on the work they are doing and the new learning they are acquiring. Each teacher becomes an action researcher and, as such, infuses the entire process of supervision and evaluation with integrity and credibility.

Naturally, the process of enacting a professional development plan is different for every teacher because each teacher's plan is unique. This chapter tells the stories of our three illustrative educators—Marcia, Eileen, and Larry—to show some of the various ways in which PBSE professional development plans may unfold.

Eileen's Story

◢ The end of January was approaching, and Principal Gary Mulholland could not believe how quickly the year was flying by. He had recently completed draft professional development plans with each faculty member; now it was time to get those plans up and running.

Where to begin? Most of his faculty had demonstrated at least a moderate comfort level with the PBSE model and had been able to create, with varying degrees of support, a professional development plan focused on improving their own ability to address identified student needs. However, there were three or four teachers who had struggled to understand the PBSE model, and working with student performance data was a particular sticking point. As experienced and conscientious educators, they were more than competent at implementing traditional instruction and assessment and at calculating marking-period and end-of-year grades. But the idea of developing different kinds of assessments and examining student data from multiple perspectives was new to them.

One of these experienced teachers was Eileen Blanchard. The work Eileen had done to draft her professional development plan had sparked her interest in PBSE and given her an idea of the impact it could have. Still, the real challenge would be implementing that plan. Gary pulled out his folder on Eileen and reviewed her plan's specific provisions (see Figure 5.4).

Gary was impressed with the work that Eileen had done, for he knew it had not been easy. He sent her a note to commend the plan and ask how things were going. He was particularly interested in finding out if she had begun looking into professional development resources, had attended the first building-level inservice seminar on data collection and analysis, and had connected with Charlie Ramirez, the district's mathematics department chairperson for grades 7–12, whom Eileen had asked to provide guidance on the development of standards-based math units and assessments.

Two weeks later, a somewhat uncomfortable Eileen stopped by Gary's office. She was running behind on her professional development plan and she knew it. Her tentative efforts to get together with Charlie Ramirez had resulted in only one meeting, which had left her feeling that she had a good deal more to learn about standards-based teaching and assessment. Eileen confided to Gary that the new learning was not coming easily, and that this was hard for her to accept.

Gary appreciated Eileen's candor. Seeing that it would be necessary to take a more active role in guiding Eileen's professional development, he suggested they get together for a three-way meeting with the district math chairperson to figure out how to get her plan back on track.

Charlie Ramirez was pleased to get Gary's call. His own leadership responsibilities and related activities had brought him extensive knowledge of standards-based curriculum, instruction, and assessment in secondary-level mathematics, but he was not sure how much the classroom teachers throughout district knew about these topics. Charlie sometimes struggled to clarify the role he should take with the middle school math teachers and had long felt that he could be of more service to them.

Charlie confirmed that he had met with Eileen in mid-November. He noted that although Eileen had listened politely as he reviewed essential learning and standards-based assessment in mathematics, she had seemed ill at ease. Most of their meeting had focused on helping Eileen develop ideas for standards-based math units. One of his recommendations was that she think of the intended outcome of each unit before creating specific lessons, so that her instruction would focus on the skills and knowledge students would need to solve complex problems related to the unit's content. Eileen seemed to have a difficult time conceptualizing this. Charlie confessed that when their meeting was complete, he had doubts that Eileen understood the PBSE model or knew what she needed to do next, despite her assurance to the contrary. He told Gary that the plan had been for Eileen to send him a draft of a standards-based unit and assessment within a month of the meeting. Those materials never arrived.

Refocusing on the Identification and Assessment of Essential Learning. Clearly, Eileen needed more support. Recognizing Charlie's content expertise, Gary asked him what advice he would give Eileen. Charlie responded that, in his opinion, Eileen needed to spend more time in a self-study on standards-based instruction and assessment. He had some materials from the National Council of Teachers of Mathematics he could send her, along with links to some high-quality online resources. Charlie also volunteered to oversee Eileen's self-study and help her gain a better understanding of how to translate the standards into holistic statements of what students needed to learn. Then he would work with her to transform those statements into performance tasks that would yield more authentic assessments of students' knowledge and skills.

In mid-January, Gary and Charlie met with Eileen to review their recommendations and seek her input. Afterward, Eileen was relieved. The work they had described was clearly relevant to her instructional responsibilities and seemed doable. Mostly, she was thankful that she would have the time to deepen her understanding of mathematics standards before trying to develop standards-based lessons and assessments. She committed to meet with Charlie each Monday after school and to work on a revised version of her professional development plan. Charlie suggested they meet in Eileen's classroom to maximize her comfort level.

In late February, Eileen scheduled a mid-cycle conference with Gary and asked Charlie to join them. After five sessions with Charlie to focus on standards-based instruction and assessment, she was beginning to feel more confident in her understanding of math standards and her understanding of how to use them effectively.

Eileen brought two documents to the meeting. The first was an outline of ideas for a unit on fractions, decimals, and percents. She had worked on this with Charlie, who had encouraged her efforts and was impressed with the results, but she wanted Gary's input as well. As Eileen presented the initial ideas and explained that the unit would evolve in the coming months, it was clear to Gary that she was not only thinking about teaching and learning in mathematics in a very different way, but beginning to apply this understanding to classroom instruction. Eileen's lesson planning was now focused more clearly on standards-based mathematics content and skills: what her students would need to know and be able to do to in order to solve complex mathematical problems. Eileen's ideas for the new unit also demonstrated her growth in understanding what constituted "essential learning."

The second document Eileen shared was a revised professional development plan (see Figure 7.1, p. 108). To reflect what had actually occurred and to provide a smooth segue into future professional development, Eileen had updated the first part of the plan. But it was the work ahead that reflected the most substantive changes. Eileen had pushed back the time frame for standards-related activities and deemphasized data collection and analysis. She would postpone sustained work on data analysis until the following academic year. As a result, the revised professional development plan focused more heavily on teacher growth than on a specific student learning objective.

To Gary, it made perfect sense for Eileen to concentrate on exploring standards-based instruction and assessment, as deep understanding in this area would be the foundation for a future exploration of performance data. He noted that the plan also provided for ongoing, sustained interaction with Charlie, the district's mathematics department chairperson. If all went well, this collaboration would result in the development of two standards-based math units. The first of these would focus on fractions, decimals, and percents and would include a performance assessment to be scored with a standards-based rubric. Gary liked the plan very much because it was responsive to Eileen's learning needs while addressing the connection between professional development and student learning.

Implementing Eileen's Professional Development Plan. Over the next several months, Eileen pursued her revised professional development plan, constituting her participation in the Secondary Monitoring Phase of the PBSE model. By mid-May, she had created, implemented, and analyzed her first fully standards-based unit. (As it turned out, the goal of developing two standards-based units was a bit ambitious; Eileen found that she needed time to really concentrate on this first unit.)

Figure 7.1
Eileen Blanchard's Professional Development Plan—Revised January 27

Plan for the Students	Time Line	Plan for the Teacher
	by October 3	• Initial meeting with supervisor to discuss PBSE.
	by October 15	• Begin broad, Web-based investigation of math standards; in particular, investigate state standards related to fractions, decimals, and percents. • Begin to gather 6th grade math scores on the state assessment.
	by October 31	• Meet with supervisor to discuss mathematics standards, state assessment scores, and hypotheses regarding potential focus for the professional development plan. • Investigate other local and statewide content experts and PD resources, activities, and readings related to math standards.
	by November 15	• Begin PD readings related to mathematics standards. • Meet with the district math department chairperson about learning how to develop standards-based math units and assessments.
	by November 30	• Determine specific standards-based knowledge and skills related to fractions, decimals, and percents (as seen through state assessment data and resources) and begin to analyze these data. • Draft a professional development plan.

	by January 20	• Meet with supervisor and the district math department chairperson to revise the professional development focus.
	by February 28	• Continue to meet weekly with the district math department chairperson regarding standards-based math assessment. • Develop an outline of a standards-based mathematics unit. • Revise the professional development plan.
• Begin teaching the standards-based unit on fractions, decimals, and percents.	by March 15	• Meet with the district math department chairperson to review drafts of the unit assessment and rubric.
• Implement a standards-based assessment on fractions, decimals, and percents. Use a standards-based rubric to score the assessment.	by April 15	• Meet with district math department chairperson to analyze the results of the unit performance assessment. • Meet with supervisor to review this analysis and share student work. • Schedule and conduct formal observations by supervisor and the district math department chairperson.
• Implement a second standards-based math unit and assessment. Use a standards-based rubric to score the assessment.	by May 15	• Develop a second standards-based math unit, assessment, and rubric. • Analyze assessment results with the district math department chairperson.
	by May 30	• Meet with supervisor and the district math department chairperson for the summative review meeting. Present student work and artifacts from the professional development plan work.

Eileen set up a meeting with Charlie and Gary to discuss her unit. As she reviewed the unit plan, assessment, rubric, and results and shared samples of student work, she detailed what her pupils had learned and what she needed to do next to extend that learning. Both the artifacts she shared and her ability to discuss them with a depth of understanding demonstrated Eileen's readiness for the professional responsibilities to be fulfilled at the end of the PBSE cycle: the Summative Review Phase.

Gary was delighted. Although Eileen would need to continue to deepen her understanding of standards, it was clear she had grown tremendously. At the end of the day, he made a special trip to Eileen's classroom to commend her efforts again and ask if she thought an observation of the work she was doing would now be appropriate. Excited to share her new learning, Eileen scheduled an observation for later that week.

The observation proved to be a timely opportunity for Gary to reinforce Eileen's efforts to ground instruction in mathematics standards and to be responsive to student learning needs. As Gary watched Eileen working with her students, he saw that she had been able to transfer her deeper understanding of math standards to her current unit of instruction. The data he collected on her performance during the observation gave him the chance to model how to use data for instructional decision making and the opportunity to isolate two or three suggestions for Eileen's continuing growth. Eileen looked forward to inviting Gary back for another observation early in the coming academic year. ◢

Reflection on Eileen's Story

In Eileen's story, we see an example of how Performance-Based Supervision and Evaluation might unfold over the course of an academic year and an illustration of one of the "individual paths" that are a hallmark of the model. It also shows how an established professional development plan may need significant modification based on the teacher's learning needs. When Eileen does not seem to make progress, Gary recognizes that the integrity of the PBSE process lies in its adherence to the principle of authenticity; that is, a teacher cannot simply go through the motions of pursuing her improvement objective. The teacher must begin where he or she actually is on the learning continuum. In Eileen's case, procrastination with her initial standards-based tasks arose not from resistance, but from a lack of confidence that she had the knowledge and skills to complete the tasks effectively. In addition, success with PBSE requires that the artifacts of student performance be authentic. If Eileen had continued with her professional development plan as originally written, her limited understanding of standards-based instruction and strategic intervention would have led her to invalid conclusions about her students' work. As Gary's actions illustrate, a supervisor's decisions about how to guide a teacher require flexibility and insight into the complex challenge of meaningful and capacity-building professional development.

Figure 7.2 (see p. 112) depicts the most substantial changes made in the second version of Eileen's professional development plan: the differentiation enacted to make her learning more timely, relevant, and effective. Moreover, the emphasis on teacher learning as a prerequisite to student learning is clear. In PBSE, maximizing the number of teacher activities and enforcing the teacher's adherence to the original plan are not the goals. What matters is what the teacher learns during his or her journey and how the teacher's capacity to craft effective instruction and assessment grows as a result.

Here are some additional reflections on Eileen's experiences that further illustrate elements of Performance-Based Supervision and Evaluation in action:

• Eileen's initial difficulty enacting her professional development plan results in delayed action and discomfort. Her supervisor sees that he and Charlie Ramirez, Eileen's expert advisor, must address both her professional learning needs and her need for emotional and moral support—and they do so by taking a more active role in the collaboration. As Eileen begins to feel less overwhelmed by the gap between her previous professional experience and the goals for her new learning, she becomes more open to engaging in the work of PBSE.

• The importance of the sustained guidance and support Eileen receives from Charlie, her advisor, cannot be overstated. Regular meetings to answer questions, model procedures, and provide feedback and encouragement help her to grow in expertise and confidence. Eileen's ability, by the mid-cycle conference, to offer ideas

Figure 7.2
A Comparison of Eileen Blanchard's Original and Revised Professional Development Plan

Month	Original Plan for the Teacher	Revised Plan for the Teacher	Original Plan for the Students	Revised Plan for the Students
October	Meet with the supervisor; investigate resources on math standards; gather math standardized scores.	Meet with supervisor; begin broad investigation of resources on math standards; gather math standardized scores.	—	—
November	Begin inservice seminar; meet with the district math department chairperson; analyze standardized performance data.	Meet with the district math department chairperson; identify fractions, decimals, and percents as target.	—	—
December	Develop and implement a trial standards-based math unit.	Continue to read and think about math standards.	Teach a trial standards-based math unit on decimals, fractions, and percents.	—
January	Develop and implement a standards-based math unit on decimals, fractions, and percents, including an assessment and rubric; analyze performance data; continue seminar.	Meet with the district math department chairperson and the supervisor to revise professional development plan.	Teach a fully developed standards-based math unit and follow with a performance-based assessment of decimals, fractions, and percents.	—

February	Mid-cycle conference; performance-based student assessment; continue professional development.	Meet weekly with district math department chairperson to outline a possible standards-based unit.	Begin instructional interventions for decimals, fractions, and percents.	—
March	Continue professional development.	Meet with the district math department chairperson and the supervisor to review drafts of the standards-based unit and assessment.	Continue instructional interventions for decimals, fractions, and percents.	Implement the first standards-based unit on decimals, fractions, and percents.
April	Meet with the district math department chairperson; develop and implement a second standards-based math unit on decimals, fractions, and percents, including a performance-based assessment and rubric; observation by supervisor.	Implement a standards-based unit and assessment and analyze it with the district math department chairperson; arrange for formal observation.	Continue instructional interventions for decimals, fractions, and percents.	Administer the first performance assessment on decimals, fractions, and percents.
May	Complete professional development activities; complete analysis of student performance data; submit artifacts of growth and discuss them at the summative review conference.	Develop, implement, and analyze a second unit and assessment with the math chairperson; conduct the summative review of artifacts and teacher growth.	Implement a second standards-based math unit and performance assessment on decimals, fractions, and percents.	Implement a second standards-based math unit and performance assessment on decimals, fractions, and percents.

about a standards-based unit of instruction is evidence that her collaboration with Charlie has helped her conceive of math instruction and assessment in a new way. Her accomplishments by the end of the year confirm the considerable benefit of their collaboration.

• A key moment in Eileen's PBSE work occurs during the May meeting, when she is able to discuss the results of the performance-based unit. She has completed the data analysis process (albeit with coaching from Charlie) and is also able to discuss the results with a modest level of understanding and an idea of how this action research data might factor into her future instructional decisions. She is indeed conducting action research, and this is a significant milepost on every teacher's PBSE journey.

• Note that Gary does not conduct a formal classroom observation of Eileen until well into the academic year. This should not be interpreted as problematic or as a supervisory deficiency. For the majority of the year, Gary chooses to supervise Eileen through informal observation and through close monitoring of both her progress in learning about standards and her ongoing collaboration with Charlie. He does not suggest a formal observation until Eileen is ready to demonstrate progress toward her objective. This allows the observation to generate authentic dialogue about Eileen's work as well as focused feedback and recommendations.

• Finally, Eileen's story depicts her transition from a teacher who begins her involvement with PBSE with some reticence into one who is taking more control over her own learning and doing so with confidence and pride.

Larry's Story

◪ In October, after his meetings with Gary to determine a focus for student learning needs and related professional development, Larry Rinaldi was ready to get started on the professional development plan he had drafted. He had already discussed his learning objective with Joan Campbell, the district's physical education department chairperson, and she was in full support of his planned initiatives.

Larry kept his draft professional development plan (see Figure 7.3) in his lesson planning book, making it easy for him to review the time line

Figure 7.3
Larry Rinaldi's Professional Development Plan

Plan for the Students	Time Line	Plan for the Teacher
	by October 3	• Initial meeting with supervisor to discuss PBSE.
	by October 10	• Begin to collect and examine student performance data on the state fitness assessment for the last four years. • Begin to gather focused PD resources related to essential learning in PE and to the collection and analysis of student performance data for instructional planning.
	by October 20	• Meet regularly with supervisor to discuss student fitness performance data. • Begin PD readings related to the collection and analysis of student fitness performance data.
	by November 1	• Begin to disaggregate the 6th grade state fitness assessment scores for each of the four subtests and among groups of students. • Meet with the district PE department chairperson regarding standards-based instruction and assessment. • Draft a professional development plan.
	by November 10	• Sign up for the building inservice seminar on the collection and analysis of student performance data. • Investigate confirming data from existing classroom assessments. If this is unavailable, draft a new classroom assessment related to the state fitness assessment.

(continued)

Figure 7.3   (*continued*)

Plan for the Students	Time Line	Plan for the Teacher
• Administer the standards-based assessment to students in 7th grade PE classes.	by November 20	• Develop a standards-based rubric that is aligned with district curriculum for assessing fitness in the target skill areas.
	by November 30	• Begin the building inservice seminar on data collection and analysis. • Using the standards-based rubric, evaluate student performance on the assessment and analyze performance data from the standards-based assessment. • Determine the cohort of students who will receive instructional interventions during "open gym" period or after school; this will be a small group (15 or so students). • Determine the specific knowledge and skills related to the targeted fitness needs.
	by December 10	• Investigate internal and external PD resources in the teaching and assessment of the specific knowledge and skills related to the targeted fitness needs. • Continue to participate in the building inservice seminar on data collection and analysis.
	by January 15	• Participate in PD activities for the teaching and assessment of the specific knowledge and skills related to the targeted fitness needs. • Draft focused interventions for the target group of students.

• Investigate statewide professional development activities, content experts, and professional readings related to the assessed fitness skills. • Continue to meet with the district PE department chairperson and other content experts regarding standards-based instruction and assessment.	by January 30	• Involve the target cohort of students in additional fitness interventions during the "open gym" period or after school. • Embed the assessed skills into all 7th grade PE classes through integration into existing units of instruction.
• Submit a mid-cycle report of progress in student learning. • Schedule and complete the mid-cycle conference with supervisor; modify the professional development plan as needed. • Continue to participate in the building inservice seminar on data collection and analysis.	by February 10	• Continue instructional interventions in the target fitness areas, modifying interventions based on continuing analysis of student performance data.
• Schedule and complete supervisor's observation of intervention lessons (in class and through additional instructional time), teacher–supervisor conferencing, and instructional adjustments. • Continue to meet with the district PE department chairperson and other content experts regarding standards-based instruction and assessment. • Develop a second assessment to monitor the progress of the target group.	by April 15	
• Complete the building inservice seminar on data collection and analysis. • Complete readings, consultations with fitness experts, and other PD activities.	by May 1	• Administer a second assessment of targeted fitness areas to the target group.
• Complete the analysis and review of the second fitness assessment data, using the same standards-based rubric.	by May 5	
• Submit results and the final report of progress to supervisor. • Schedule and complete summary conference and reflect on the year's professional development plan.	by May 20	

periodically and note tasks to be completed and resources to be investigated. This system also helped Larry make explicit connections between his professional development and new instructional initiatives.

Using Data to Determine Student Learning Needs. Larry's initial data analysis (see Chapter 5) had indicated that Fairview's 6th and 8th grade students could certainly become more fit—the girls in particular. The first step in his plan was to obtain updated information on his students' current fitness levels and then try his hand at creating a standards-based rubric by which to measure their progress over the upcoming months.

The state physical fitness assessment was administered to students in grades 4, 6, 8, and 10, and Larry decided to focus on 7th graders. He reasoned that an "off year" snapshot of performance would generate baseline data for interventions before the students' next state assessment. With the help of Joan, the department chairperson, Larry modeled his classroom assessment after the four tests in the state assessment:

- A partial curl-up test to measure strength and endurance;
- A right-angle push-up test to measure upper body strength;
- A one-mile run/walk to measure aerobic endurance; and
- A modified sit and reach test to measure flexibility.

To determine student performance, Larry looked to the state guidelines, which provided cutoff points for student performance at two levels of fitness: "health," representing a healthy level of fitness for children in each age bracket; and "challenge," describing children with exceptional fitness and skills. This was a good beginning, but because Larry needed to measure the status and progress of students who fell below—sometimes far below—the state's "health" level, he created three new levels: "nearly health," "below health," and "significantly below health." Using the state cutoff points as a foundation, Larry determined proportional benchmarks for his new levels by developing an incremental scale for each of the tests. Finally, as the state had done, he created separate rubrics for boys and girls (see Figure 7.4).

Pleased with this work, Larry shared his rubrics with his advisor, Joan. She concurred that the benchmarks he had determined were both reasonable and useful. Larry had created standards-based rubrics and could now monitor the progress of less-fit students against a common set of measures and encourage the students to set personal fitness goals.

By mid-November, Larry had administered the classroom assessment to all 192 of his 7th graders. Before meeting with Gary to share the results, he constructed a table to facilitate data analysis (see Figure 7.5, p. 120).

The data were a revelation. All the state fitness assessment reports Larry had ever seen presented information in the same manner: as the number and percent of students who met proficiency levels and the number and percent who did not. Larry's rubrics gave him a new way to

Figure 7.4
Fitness-Level Benchmarks for 7th Grade Boys and Girls

1. Rubric for Boys

Fitness Level	One-Mile Walk/Run (min/sec)		Sit and Reach (cm)		Right-Angle Push-Ups (#)		Curl-Ups (#)	
	Age 12	*Age 13*	*Age 12*	*Age 13*	*Age 12*	*Age 13*	*Age 12*	*Age 13*
Challenge	7:15*	7:00*	33*	33*	24*	25*	55*	59*
Health	9:00*	8:30*	25*	25*	12*	13*	28*	30*
Nearly Health	10:45	10:00	22	22	10	11	24	26
Below Health	12:30	11:30	18	18	8	9	20	22
Significantly Below Health	14:15	13:00	15	15	6	7	16	18

2. Rubric for Girls

Fitness Level	One-Mile Walk/Run (min/sec)		Sit and Reach (cm)		Right-Angle Push-Ups (#)		Curl-Ups (#)	
	Age 12	*Age 13*	*Age 12*	*Age 13*	*Age 12*	*Age 13*	*Age 12*	*Age 13*
Challenge	8:30*	8:15*	38*	39*	17*	18*	52*	55*
Health	10:15*	10:00*	26*	27*	8*	8*	26*	28*
Nearly Health	12:00	11:45	23	24	6	6	22	24
Below Health	13:45	13:30	20	21	4	4	18	20
Significantly Below Health	15:30	15:15	17	18	2	2	14	16

*Source: Connecticut State Department of Education (n.d.).

examine that information and showed him that most of the students who did not meet proficiency levels were in the "nearly health" range, while a fairly consistent but small group fell into the "below health" or "significantly below health" ranges. In almost every category, boys achieved higher fitness levels than girls, and the difference was even more apparent for push-ups, an indicator of upper body strength.

Larry scheduled a meeting with Gary and Joan. To prepare for their discussion, he gathered descriptions of the standards he had assessed, his classroom assessment and rubrics, a summary of student performance on his assessment, and a list of individual students and their fitness scores.

Figure 7.5

Fitness-Level Results for 7th Grade Boys and Girls

Fitness Level	One-Mile Walk/Run (min/sec)		Sit and Reach (cm)		Right-Angle Push-Ups (#)		Curl-Ups (#)	
	Boys	Girls	Boys	Girls	Boys	Girls	Boys	Girls
Challenge	18 (19%)	9 (9%)	16 (17%)	18 (18%)	22 (23%)	2 (2%)	19 (20%)	18 (18%)
Health	41 (44%)	36 (37%)	42 (45%)	47 (48%)	43 (46%)	30 (31%)	45 (48%)	42 (43%)
Nearly Health	26 (28%)	38 (39%)	25 (27%)	22 (22%)	24 (26%)	37 (38%)	22 (24%)	22 (22%)
Below Health	5 (5%)	10 (10%)	7 (7%)	8 (8%)	3 (3%)	21 (21%)	5 (5%)	12 (12%)
Significantly Below Health	4 (4%)	5 (5%)	4 (4%)	3 (3%)	2 (2%)	8 (8%)	3 (3%)	4 (4%)

N = 192 (94 boys, 98 girls)

In each area of fitness, a number of students had scored below or significantly below the health level: as few as 5 and as many as 11 boys, and as few as 11 and as many as 29 girls. Eleven girls had scored below or significantly below health level in *all four* areas of fitness.

Larry was pleased to be able to organize, array, and present his data in different ways because he knew it would enrich the conversation at his meeting. It was particularly gratifying because he had always thought that the appropriate response to standardized test information was to look at the lowest general areas of performance and use these as the basis for supplementary lessons and activities in all of his classes. Now he could see that among 7th graders, there were 11 students who clearly needed his attention more than others, and that intervention was necessary in multiple elements of fitness. Larry decided to draft a student learning objective:

Students identified as "below health" or "significantly below health" on all four areas of their fall fitness assessment will improve by at least one level in each of the four areas of fitness by June 15 of this school year.

Implementing Larry's Professional Development Plan. At their meeting, Gary and Joan concurred with Larry's recommendation that he focus on the identified group of 11 girls. Because this was an entirely new way of working for Larry, he asked for some extra time so that he could approach interventions with the students carefully. He explained that he wanted to use December and January to do the following:

• Research current best practice in addressing strength, endurance, and flexibility.

• Seek out appropriate inservice opportunities related to his focus, especially from a gendered perspective.

• Develop individualized lessons for the target students.

• Meet with the target students and their parents to gain their commitment to the extra instruction.

• Enrich his physical education library with additional materials.

• Continue attending the building-level seminar program on data collection and analysis, as what he had already learned in this program had been very valuable.

His plan received full approval from Joan and Gary.

By the end of the January, Larry had completed most of the professional development activities and instructional planning he needed, and was ready to begin interventions with his targeted students. With Gary and Joan's approval and encouragement, he created the "Fitness Club" as a way to put a positive spin on his interventions. Nine of the 11 girls invited to this club made a commitment to join. He began to meet with them as a group during the activity period at the end of the school day, and to meet with them individually during segments of their recess period. Using the state physical fitness standards as a model, Larry encouraged each girl to keep a journal to record daily physical activities and to log her progress in activities that supported strength, endurance, and flexibility.

To monitor the progress of the Fitness Club members, Larry created four standards-based classroom assessments to be administered throughout the remainder of the year. He also developed a data collection form that he could use to record the results of these ongoing assessments and plan future instruction. Using the girls' rubric, which he had based on the state's model (see Figure 7.4), Larry developed a system for recording the progress of each student in his intervention group over time, with numbers corresponding to the five levels of fitness. By mid-February, his tracking form already charted two sets of performance data for his targeted students (see Figure 7.6, p. 122).

Collaborative Conversation to Improve Student Learning. In late February, Larry shared the artifacts of his work with Gary and Joan at his mid-cycle review conference. As they listened to Larry's discussion of his assessment, rubrics, data analysis sheets, lessons, and student journals, it was clear that he understood the substance and process of Performance-Based Supervision and Evaluation. Furthermore, Gary saw that Larry had been able to use PBSE strategies—such as the four tests and the examination

Figure 7.6
Longitudinal Tracking Form for Fitness Club Performance Data

Student Name	One-Mile Walk/Run				Sit and Reach				Right-Angle Push-Ups				Curl-Ups			
	Nov	Feb	Apr	June	Nov	Feb	Apr	June	Nov	Feb	Apr	June	Nov	Feb	Apr	June
Amanda	1	1			1	1			1	1			1	1		
Courtney	2	2			2	3			2	2			2	2		
Gabby	2	2			2	3			1	2			2	2		
Irina	1	1			2	2			1	1			1	1		
Keisha	1	1			1	2			1	1			1	2		
Phoenix	2	2			2	2			1	2			2	2		
Selena	2	2			2	2			1	1			2	2		
Tamika	1	2			2	2			1	1			2	2		
Wanda	1	1			1	2			1	1			1	1		

Scale: 5 = Challenge Level; 4 = Health Level; 3 = Nearly Health Level; 2 = Below Health Level; 1 = Significantly Below Health Level and analysis of student data—in different ways to identify precise student learning needs within the mountain of data he had at his disposal. Given the brief duration of Larry's interventions with the target students, there were minimal performance data demonstrating progress. Nonetheless, Larry was able to discuss his work clearly and articulate its growing influence on his students' attitudes and activity levels. Gary knew that Larry was now functioning as an action researcher in his approach to teaching and learning.

Joan and Gary recommended that Larry continue with his efforts through the end of the year, administering two more classroom assessments to monitor the progress of his students and making necessary adjustments to his instructional interventions. For their part, they would continue to support Larry's new learning and suggest other ways he might improve instruction and assessment throughout this Secondary Monitoring Phase of the PBSE process.

During the spring, both Gary and Joan formally observed Larry working with a Fitness Club member and offered feedback. In addition, Gary conducted informal walk-through observations during a number of activity periods to watch Larry working with the full membership of the Fitness Club. After each visit, Gary never failed to commend Larry's work and encourage him to continue. ◪

Reflection on Larry's Story

Although Larry adapted to Performance-Based Supervision and Evaluation more smoothly than Eileen did, at the outset, he had much to learn before he felt comfortable with and confident in his ability to approach teaching and learning in this different way. Several important points emerge from Larry's experience:

• Like a typical "data-prolific" teacher, Larry enters the PBSE process already extremely conscientious about monitoring student performance and collecting a lot of data to be sure that he has multiple ways of knowing how his students are doing. He knows how to aggregate these data and look across performances to identify the status of an individual student, but lacks the analytical tools to break the data apart to reveal common instructional needs for subgroups of students. Disaggregating student performance data and looking at them from different perspectives are the teacher's fundamental tools for planning instruction (indicators TP-3 and TP-4 in the Teacher Preparation Phase of the Criteria of Excellence).

• Larry is accustomed to trying his best to address the needs of all his physical education students. His past efforts to provide additional and even remedial instruction were always within the context of whole-group teaching. After all, if he focused on just a few students, wouldn't the others miss out on the extra learning experiences? For Larry, it is difficult to let the data frame decisions about which students need support and what that support should be. With the help of Gary's "permission" to go ahead and focus intervention on just a few students, along with his own growing ability to explore student performance data, Larry is able to transition from "macro-instruction" to "micro-instruction."

• Larry's fairly strong aptitude for working with data and his previous experience collecting student performance information through multiple sources support his new learning in PBSE. As a result, while he certainly benefits from the commendations and encouragement provided by his principal and district department chairperson, he does not require intense and ongoing moral support to achieve his professional learning goals.

• What establishes Larry as an action researcher is not only his ability to collect and analyze data, but his growing ability to explain the data and identify implications for teaching and learning. With additional experience, Larry may quickly become a peer resource for other teachers in his building.

Marcia's Story

⬛ Early in November, Gary decided to send a note to Marcia Williams. He had been impressed by her quick grasp of Performance-Based Supervision and Evaluation and how she had translated what she had picked up during the inservice activities into professional action.

Like her colleague Larry Rinaldi, Marcia kept her professional development plan in her planning book for easy reference and integration into her long- and short-term plans (see Figure 7.7).

Implementing Marcia's Professional Development Plan. Early in her experiences with PBSE, Marcia demonstrated the ability to enhance her

Figure 7.7
Marcia Williams's Professional Development Plan

Plan for the Students	Time Line	Plan for the Teacher
	by September 15	• Investigate state standards for writing, especially persuasive writing. • Contact the building writing expert to seek support in developing an assessment to collect confirming data.
	by October 1	• Develop a writing assessment instrument for baseline data. • Develop a standards-based rubric for the assessment. • Sign up for the fall districtwide inservice course on standards-based writing instruction.
• Administer a baseline writing assessment.	by October 10	• Continue to investigate PD resources for writing instruction and assessment.
	by October 20	• Complete an analysis of the baseline assessment; identify the group of students for intervention. • Ask the building writing expert for informal coaching on writing instruction and assessment. • Begin the fall districtwide inservice course on standards-based writing instruction.
	by October 30	• Complete a teacher–supervisor review of student performance data and discuss the focus of the professional development plan.
	by October 31	• Complete an initial search for PD resources; acquire resource materials (books, articles, guides, etc.) for teaching and assessing the writing skills of elaboration and comprehensiveness, particularly in persuasive writing. • Complete a draft professional development plan.
	by November 15	• Review acquired resource materials and complete draft lesson plans for instructional interventions. • Review and revise these lesson plans with supervisor.
• Begin implementing intervention lessons with a focus on elaboration and comprehensiveness in persuasive writing with the target group of students.	by November 20	• Continue participation in the district inservice course on standards-based writing instruction.

(continued)

Figure 7.7 (*continued*)

Plan for the Students	Time Line	Plan for the Teacher
• Administer an intermediate writing assessment to the intervention group, focusing on elaboration and comprehensiveness.	by January 5	• Develop an intermediate assessment to be used with the previously developed persuasive writing rubric.
	by January 15	• Update list of PD resources related to elaboration and comprehensiveness in persuasive writing. • Sign up for the district's spring course on standards-based assessment.
	by January 20	• Analyze and review the intermediate writing assessment; make necessary changes to instructional interventions.
• Continue instructional interventions for elaboration and comprehensiveness in persuasive writing, modified based on analysis of the performance data.	by February 1	• Submit a mid-cycle report of progress in student learning to supervisor. • Complete the mid-cycle conference with supervisor; modify professional development plan as needed. • Begin district course on standards-based assessment.
	by April 15	• Schedule and complete the supervisor's observation of intervention lessons, teacher–supervisor post-observation conferencing, and instructional adjustments.
• Administer a summative writing assessment to intervention group. • Ask involved students to write a personal reflection about their learning as a member of the intervention group.	by May 1	• Complete readings, consultations with writing experts, and other PD activities.
	by May 5	• Complete an analysis and review of summative assessment data, including student comments.
	by May 20	• Submit results and a final report of progress to supervisor. • Schedule and complete the summative conference and reflect on the year's professional development plan.

own learning. Fairly independently, she identified essential knowledge and skills, developed a data-based focus on the teaching of persuasive writing, and completed a useful baseline assessment of student skills. Based on these efforts and her obvious initiative, Gary felt comfortable encouraging Marcia to direct her own professional development activities over the next three months. He suggested that they meet for a mid-cycle review of her interim assessment of student writing, but reassured her that he would be available and very happy to help should she need support at any time.

Halfway through the month of January, Marcia requested a meeting with Gary. A bit embarrassed, she apologized for the delay in producing the information they had agreed to discuss at the mid-cycle conference. Marcia had administered an interim writing assessment just after the holiday break and had attempted to evaluate it with the persuasive writing rubric she had constructed in the fall. Despite her prior successful use of the rubric, this time she had encountered papers that she was not sure how to score. Marcia explained that she had asked a colleague, an experienced 8th grade language arts teacher, to look at the problematic papers and try to apply the rubric. Because of this, she needed more time to complete the scoring process and prepare for her conference.

To Marcia's surprise, Gary was pleased. He reassured Marcia that these decisions she was making about assessment, validity, and reliability were a sign of her maturing understanding of Performance-Based Supervision and Evaluation. She was now thinking deeply about student learning and more deeply about how to apply a rubric to student performances than she had been when she first assessed her students' writing skills. Gary not only approved Marcia's request for an extension, he suggested that she ask her language arts colleague to read and score all the papers, not just the problematic ones; this would give her a truly reliable and paired set of scores. He assured Marcia that doing this would be a valuable professional development experience. He even offered to provide substitute teachers for Marcia and her colleague so that they could do this work within in the context of a normal workday and have time to discuss those papers about which they had arrived at disparate judgments. Marcia appreciated Gary's support and saw his invitation as an opportunity to extend her capacity as not only a social studies teacher, but as a teacher who would be able to support her students' writing skills through integrated instruction and assessment.

Collaborative Conversation to Improve Student Learning. Despite Gary's invitation to take as much time as she needed, Marcia was ready to discuss her work and how it had affected student learning at a mid-cycle conference in late February. Her presentation of student work, analysis of progress, and ideas for future instruction were timely and appropriate. One of the artifacts Marcia shared was a data-monitoring sheet she had created to track her targeted students' progress (see Figure 7.8). For purposes of data collection, Marcia focused on the two areas of standards identified by her improvement objective, Support and Detail, and Comprehensiveness.

The gains made since the first assessment in October clearly demonstrated that some of Marcia's students had made progress, particularly in the area of Support and Detail. Nonetheless, there was still work to be done. Marcia concluded her mid-cycle conference by inviting Gary to see firsthand the strategies she was using to improve her students' writing skills.

The classroom observation confirmed Marcia's considerable contribution to the 8th grade team's effort to address student writing skills. Gary encouraged Marcia to continue her professional development initiatives and to continue to apply her new learning to classroom instruction in persuasive writing through the second half of the school year. ◢

Figure 7.8
Targeted Students' Progress on Persuasive Writing Skills—January

Student Name	Support and Detail			Comprehensiveness		
	Oct	Jan*	May	Oct	Jan*	May
Maggie	3	4		3	4	
George	3	3		3	3	
Miguel	2	3		3	3	
Tanya	2	4		3	4	
Zachary	2	3		3	3	
Ethan	3	4		3	3	
Matt	2	3		2	3	
Jasmine	3	3		3	3	
Jim	2	3		3	4	
Candace	3	4		3	3	
Jose	2	3		2	2	

*Consensus score derived through discussion with the 8th grade language arts teacher.
Note: Writing was scored on a rubric of 6 (Well-Developed) to 1 (Undeveloped); 4 = Proficient.

Reflection on Marcia's Story

Marcia Williams stands out as a teacher who epitomizes the action researcher and who consistently holds her work to the highest standards. Through her efforts to learn more about standards-based writing instruction and use that knowledge to improve her students' writing skills, Marcia demonstrates how educators can use the PBSE process to direct their work through the Initial Monitoring, Mid-Cycle Review, and Secondary Monitoring Phases of the Criteria of Excellence.

Many of the educators with whom we have worked are as dedicated and hardworking as Marcia, and just as predisposed to work that directly improves student learning. Although Marcia's story depicts a teacher who is all this plus a quick study in Performance-Based Supervision and Evaluation, she also is a reminder that supervisors will encounter Marcia-like educators and must be prepared to challenge them and extend their learning. This means that supervisors must also take charge of their own professional development, both in Performance-Based Supervision and Evaluation and in current best practices in curriculum, instruction, and assessment.

A Few Final Thoughts on Professional Development Plan Implementation

You have now seen how three teachers might use the PBSE professional development plan to guide new learning and instructional initiatives. Although Marcia, Eileen, and Larry represent diverse focuses and experiences, they are only three case studies; among the full faculty at any school there are as many stories and journeys as there are educators. What we want to stress is that the PBSE model can improve the capacity of every teacher in any school because it is built for differentiation.

─────────────── ▽ KEYSTONE ───────────────

Performance-Based Supervision and Evaluation requires that the content and the process of each professional development plan be tailored to the individual needs of the teacher and the targeted students, and that each plan be flexible enough to change as these needs are clarified and the resources for growth are established.

Every school has its "go to" teachers—those who are very involved with responsibilities beyond the classroom or who are perceived as "experts" in curriculum, instruction, and assessment. Too often these teachers become overextended while others feel left out and undervalued. Over time, the learning that occurs through Performance-Based Supervision and Evaluation establishes every faculty member as an expert as a result of their professional development path. Each develops into a valuable resource for knowledge and skills, and, in our experience, many even become cheerleaders for the process.

8

Evaluating Teacher Growth and Development

All school administrators are required to conduct periodic and systematic formal evaluations of their teaching staff. Typically, this process follows a predetermined calendar, often calling for nontenured teachers be evaluated earlier in the academic year than tenured staff. Regardless of when they are held, all formal evaluations share a key characteristic: they make a statement about an individual's performance and value to the organization at a given point in time.

We believe that the traditional professional development cycle, which asks the teacher to set a professional goal at the beginning of the school year and report on their achievements at the end of the year, is at odds with research findings on how adults learn. Like all adult learners, teachers need to connect new learning to previous learning; to develop deep understanding of new content and skills; to receive relevant feedback about the application of their new learning; to have the opportunity to interact with colleagues as a learning community; and to view their professional development activities as part of meaningful, lifelong learning (Bransford, Brown, & Cocking, 2000). It makes no sense to assume that authentic growth and development will always occur neatly within the typical calendar for professional development and teacher evaluation.

Performance-Based Supervision and Evaluation is based on the notion that a full cycle of teacher growth is represented by both authentic improvement in teaching and evidence of improved student learning. Although each teacher creates a chronological professional development plan as a roadmap for growth, the plan's time frame reflects and responds to the teacher's learning needs.

—————————— ▽ KEYSTONE ——————————

The success of a PBSE learning cycle is measured by the quality of the teacher's development, not by the number of professional development tasks accomplished over the course of a single academic year.

Using the Criteria of Excellence to Monitor Teacher Growth

As discussed and illustrated in Chapter 7, a teacher's professional development plan guides him or her through the process of acquiring new learning and translating it into instruction and assessment practices that further student learning. Throughout, the PBSE supervisor uses the Criteria of Excellence to capture snapshots of every teacher's capacity and present a record of every teacher's growth. Let's revisit the journey of our mathematics teacher, Eileen Blanchard, to see how a supervisor can use the Criteria of Excellence in this way.

◢ For Eileen, the foundation of PBSE—understanding and using a standards-based approach to curriculum, instruction, and assessment—had been somewhat difficult to grasp at first. She knew from her own work over the years that fractions, decimals, and percents were a perennial area of lower performance for her 7th graders, but beyond the teaching methods she had used for years, she was uncertain about how to improve her students' knowledge and skills.

Gary's first evaluation of Eileen's skill competencies relative to the Criteria of Excellence placed her within the Teacher Preparation Phase. He noted her emerging capacity to identify essential and standards-based student performance data (TP-1) and judged her to be "just beginning" her work on the other indicators within the phase (see Figure 5.1).

At Gary's suggestion, Eileen put together some charts depicting student performance on standardized tests (see Figures 5.2 and 5.3), and these verified that fractions, decimals, and percents were an area of lower performance. Eileen's need for support during the data-gathering and analysis confirmed for Gary that her skills on the first indicator in the Teacher Preparation Phase (TP-1) were at an emerging level. For Eileen to develop the additional competencies to make a real impact on student learning, she first needed to learn more about standards-based curriculum, instruction, and assessment, as well as how to use data to inform instruction. Accordingly, the professional development plan she drafted focused on the elements of the Teacher Preparation Phase rather than on more advanced phases of the Criteria of Excellence (see Figure 7.1). When Eileen submitted the plan, Gary copied his assessments of Eileen's current competencies into a modified version of the Teacher Preparation Phase of the Criteria of Excellence (see Figure 8.1, p. 134). He would use this form throughout the year to monitor her progress.

Gary updated his progress notes on Eileen in late February, after she presented her modified professional development plan at the mid-cycle review meeting. In his judgment, she had definitely increased her capacity to identify standards-based student performance data (TP-1), and Gary recorded the new rating for this indicator as "competent." Eileen was also making progress on understanding holistic assessment of student knowledge (TP-2), which he now rated as "emergent."

Gary updated his notes on Eileen's progress again in mid-April and late May. His new assessment took into account the evidence of skill and understanding he'd seen in meetings with Eileen and Charlie Ramirez, the classroom observation, informal visits to Eileen's classroom, and his review of the artifacts Eileen had created and collected while pursuing her professional development plan. In his view, Eileen had grown in her ability to describe aspects of her students' learning (TP-1) and to use their work as a basis for her judgments (TP-2). She was just beginning to learn how to develop instructional interventions to address their learning needs (TP-7). All together, he had created a record of Eileen's evolving professional competencies relative to the Teacher Preparation Phase of the Criteria of Excellence. ◢

The Criteria of Excellence not only serve as a tool supervisors can use to monitor teacher growth and note judgments about developing professional competencies, but they also give supervisors the means to interface the PBSE process with district evaluation requirements. At any point during the school year, the supervisor can report specific, informed assessment about teacher performance.

Figure 8.1
Supervisor's Longitudinal Progress Notes on Eileen Blanchard—
Teacher Preparation Phase

Indicator	Criteria	Oct	Feb	Apr	May
	The teacher has identified				
TP-1	• Student performance data that represent "essential learning" and are standards-based.	E	C	C	C
TP-2	• Student performance data that result from holistic assessment of a learning task requiring students to apply multiple skills and various knowledge.	JB	E	E	C
	The teacher has organized				
TP-3	• Student performance data so that they may be viewed and interpreted in more than one way.	JB	JB	E	E
TP-4	• Student performance data to reveal student performance strengths and weaknesses.	JB	JB	E	E
	The teacher has completed an analysis of data, producing				
TP-5	• Some conclusions about student performance strengths and weaknesses.	JB	JB	E	E
TP-6	• Some artifacts of student work exemplifying student performance strengths and weaknesses.	JB	JB	E	E
TP-7	• Some ideas about how to modify teaching to bring about improved student learning in the areas targeted in the data analysis.	JB	JB	JB	JB

Evaluation Scale: C = Competent; E = Emergent; JB = Just Beginning

PBSE and the Summative Evaluation Process

How do principals like Gary Mulholland meet a district's requirements for formal, end-of-year evaluations within the context of Performance-Based Supervision and Evaluation? As you might suspect, it's by returning to the Criteria of Excellence, specifically to the Summative Review Phase (see Figure A.6 in Appendix A, p. 194). Regardless of where individual faculty members are on elements of other phases, at the end of the school year, all should complete the process requirements of the Summative Review Phase to the maximum extent possible.

Although the Summative Review Phase incorporates traditional aspects of formal evaluation—a teacher-provided update on progress to date, the supervisor's final evaluation summary report, and a meeting to sign off on the final report—elements of the PBSE model color both the context for these activities and their purpose. This is most evident in two of its distinguishing features: (1) the fact that the teacher takes the lead by submitting a final report of progress, which includes a substantive written reflection analyzing work to date and suggesting ideas for future growth; and (2) the requirement that the teacher present artifacts to substantiate that report and serve as the data-oriented basis for the conference's discussion.

 KEYSTONE

The Summative Review Phase of the Criteria of Excellence serves as a template for the formal review of teacher growth and development. Adherence to the common set of elements in this phase, with thoughtful exception for teachers whose work does not fit this format, provides a comparable base for evaluative judgments and ensures compliance with district evaluation plans and responsiveness to any regulations determined through collective bargaining.

Summative Review in Action: Eileen's Story

Eileen Blanchard's summative evaluation experience represents one teacher's pathway through the PBSE process and highlights both the professional and personal benefits the model can bring to the educators who follow it.

◪ In early May, Gary Mulholland was beginning to think about the end-of-year evaluations. Per the reminder on his annual calendar, Gary sent a memo to his certified staff, asking them begin their preparations.

By the end of the month, Eileen was ready for her summative review conference with Gary. As was the case at mid-cycle, she chose to invite Charlie Ramirez, the district's math department chairperson for grades 7–12 and her expert advisor on standards-based mathematic instruction and assessment. Over the past several months, she and Charlie had developed a strong professional relationship, and she thought it only right that he be there. For Charlie, providing ongoing support for Eileen's learning had been a win–win situation. He felt that he was finally making a direct contribution to the knowledge and skill development of one of the middle school math teachers. He also appreciated the opportunity PBSE had afforded him to collaborate with Gary Mulholland. The work they'd done together had strengthened their professional relationship as instructional leaders.

At her summative review conference, Eileen shared a number of artifacts*, and she did so with pride because they served as evidence of her hard work and achievement during the year. These included the following:

- Notes from her readings about math standards.
- A detailed memo outlining key math resources she had found during an Internet investigation.
- Notes from her meetings with Charlie.
- Her new standards-based math unit, assessment, and rubric.
- An analysis of student performance and samples of student work.
- A written professional reflection on her learning throughout the year.

Of all of these artifacts, the one that most impressed Gary was Eileen's written reflection. She acknowledged that she still had room for growth when it came to expertise in and confidence about standards-based instruction and assessment. Nonetheless, she knew that she was now thinking about her work in a very different way. In her reflection, Eileen

---

*A complete set of Eileen's artifacts is available in Appendix B, beginning on p. 197.

noted that the instructional changes she had begun to make had had an observable effect on her students. When she gave them rubrics that outlined the unit's knowledge and skills, they approached their assignments more confidently, self-assessed their work more capably, and had more success with the unit overall. In addition, Eileen noted that she had begun to think about her professional development focus for the next academic year. She wanted to further her learning about standards-based instruction and performance assessment and to begin to learn about analyzing student performance data and making data-based instructional decisions.

Gary knew he had substantive evidence of Eileen's professional growth. He had seen her expand her understanding of mathematics standards, instructional pedagogy, and authentic assessment. And although Eileen's professional development plan had been refocused on skills associated with the indicators in the first phase of the Criteria of Excellence (the Teacher Preparation Phase), she was still able to complete the more procedural Mid-Cycle Review and Summative Review Phases by reporting on her professional growth efforts, her new learning, and how both had begun to influence her classroom instruction and student learning.

Gary looked forward to writing a substantive and meaningful summative evaluation report commending Eileen's progress and recommending future professional development opportunities in the areas she had identified. Given the growth that Eileen had demonstrated, he expected that she would achieve competency in all of the indicators within the Teacher Preparation Phase of the Criteria of Excellence during the next year and begin focusing more directly on the Initial Collaboration Phase. ◢

Components of the Summative Evaluation Process

Let's take a closer look at components of the summative evaluation process found in Eileen's story.

First, you'll notice that Gary initiates the process. To experienced administrators, this course of action should look familiar. A memo (see Figure 8.2, p. 138) is sent to all professional staff members requesting that they schedule a meeting with the supervisor to review their progress to date on their professional improvement objective. The teacher prepares a final report of progress and assembles a collection of artifacts that serve as evidence of the teacher's growth to date. These two components are the jumping-off point for the summative evaluation conference, and, along with the teacher's discussion the during the conference and the supervisor's own

Figure 8.2
Summative Review Notification Memo

Date: May 1

To: Fairview Middle School Professional Staff Members

From: Gary Mulholland, Principal

Re: Summative Review

As I am sure you are aware, our district evaluation plan requires that all professional staff members be evaluated by their supervisors by July 1 of each year.

I ask that each Fairview faculty member do the following by *May 15:*

1. Gather artifacts of progress on your professional development plan this year and develop a written reflection about this growth. For your convenience, I've attached a copy of the form for this written reflection—the "Professional Development Plan: Final Report of Progress"—to this memo.

2. Schedule two appointments with your primary supervisor:
   • *The Summative Review Conference.* At this meeting, plan to review your progress and written reflection with your supervisor. This meeting will take about 45 minutes and should occur by *June 1.*
   • A follow-up meeting to discuss and sign your supervisor's written summative evaluation. This meeting should take no more than 15 minutes and should occur by *June 15.*

The summative review is the culmination of a great deal of effort expended throughout the year, and it represents the growing instructional capacity of both you and our school. I appreciate the effort that you will put into preparing your final reflection, and my fellow administrators and I are ready to assist you as you prepare to share your professional growth and development. Please do not hesitate to ask for assistance.

Thanks to all of you for the many professional development achievements you have made this year, all of which ultimately benefit our students.

collection of evidence, they inform the development of a summative evaluation report.

The Teacher's Final Report of Progress

Note that Gary's notification memo mentions a standard form for the teachers' final report of progress. Although some PBSE schools may not opt to use a common form, each teacher's report should include the following elements:

1. A statement of the objective selected by the teacher for the professional development plan. This is the focus for improvement that represents an area of essential learning identified from student performance data.

2. A brief description of the teacher's accomplishments related to the professional development plan. It is critical to the legitimacy of this description that the teacher report only those accomplishments that can be authenticated through the attached artifacts.

3. A written reflection discussing the teacher's professional growth relative to the focus of the plan.

4. A discussion of student performance data related to the teacher's professional development focus.

5. Ideas for future professional development, based on student learning needs.

Figure 8.3 (see p. 140) shows Eileen's final report of progress.

The Artifacts

The value of the artifacts in summative evaluation cannot be underestimated. They serve as the foundation for the teacher's written reflection and the basis for the summative conference. They also meet the need for accountability. Artifacts may include notes regarding professional reading or attendance at professional development workshops, examples of student work, analyses of student

Figure 8.3
Eileen Blanchard's Final Report of Progress

Staff Member: Eileen Blanchard   School Year: 2005–2006
Primary Instructional Assignment: 7th Grade Mathematics
Secondary Instructional Assignment: None
Primary Supervisor: Gary Mulholland, Principal

SECTION I: REPORT OF PROFESSIONAL GROWTH AND IMPROVEMENT

A. Statement of the Improvement Objective for Your Current Professional Development Plan

I identified a need for my mathematics students to improve their abilities to solve complex problems involving fractions, decimals, and percents. My current professional development efforts are directed toward learning more about teaching and assessment methods in order to improve my teaching in these areas.

B. Review of the Most Current Professional Development Plan and Accomplishments

My complete professional development plan is attached: Yes: X   No:

Summary of Accomplishments
Briefly describe your most significant professional development accomplishments this year, with a reference to the artifacts of evidence that are attached. Summarize only those accomplishments for which you have supporting evidence and include a reference to specific artifacts. Please do not provide detail in this section; your artifacts will provide the detail. Present accomplishments in chronological order.

10/31. I completed a Web-based investigation of math standards related to fractions, decimals, and percents, increasing my understanding of how they determine what is "essential" for students to learn. (See "Summary of Web Search on Math Standards.")

2/12. I completed specific readings about math standards, which included the review of some literature describing the connections between standards and the state mastery test. (See "Memo to the District Chairperson," and "Summary of Professional Development Readings.")

2/22. I completed an initial outline of a standards-based unit in math, which was reviewed and later approved by the principal and the district mathematics department chairperson. (See "Overview of a Standards-Based Mathematics Unit.")

Figure 8.3 *(continued)*

4/15. I completed the writing of a standards-based unit in fractions, decimals, and percents, including performance assessments and rubrics, which was ready for use in the classroom and approved by the district mathematics department chairperson. (See "Professional Reflection on a Standards-Based Mathematics Unit on Fractions, Decimals, and Percents" and "A Standards-Based Mathematics Unit on Fractions, Decimals, and Percents.")

5/20. I completed a summary report of the assessment results after teaching the standards-based math unit I developed. The summary presented an analysis of performance data and my reflections on them. (See "Analysis of and Reflections on a Standards-Based Mathematics Unit" and "Examples of Student Work.")

5/20. I completed a log of my meetings and consultations with my district chairperson, complete with reflections. These meetings occurred from November through May. (See "Log of Meetings and Reflections on Collaboration Efforts.")

SECTION II. REFLECTION ON PROFESSIONAL GROWTH AND DEVELOPMENT

Summative Reflection

When I identified the area of fractions, decimals, and percents as one in which my students could improve, I did so without really thinking much about it. In my experience as a teacher, my fellow teachers and I have always had to find some area to work on for our professional development. I knew from the state mastery test results, that fractions, decimals, and percents were areas that continue to give students difficulty, so I figured I would look into it. What I did not realize at the time was that it is not enough to simply teach students about fractions, decimals, and percents so they "get it" well enough to pass my test at the end of the unit. Honestly, that is the way I had always looked at it. After my professional development work this year, which helped me to really understand what standards are, I now realize that students must learn about fractions, decimals, and percents deeply enough to be able to apply them in complicated and real-life problems. To simply do isolated examples correctly on a test is not enough.

This new understanding and appreciation of what it means for students to learn essential knowledge and skills did not come quickly or easily. I really struggled this past fall with understanding the difference between the way I always taught math and the way I am beginning to see that it needs to be taught. I really appreciate the patience and guidance offered by my principal and district chairperson, Charlie Ramirez. With their help, and with the tremendous amount I

(continued)

Figure 8.3 (*continued*)

---

learned from professional reading, I experienced one of the biggest shifts in my teaching career.

What really convinced me that this new approach to professional development was working was when I taught a unit on fractions, decimals, and percents this spring. I had developed the unit differently and had focused on what the standards say students need to know. After teaching it, I tested students by giving them a performance assessment I developed with Charlie Ramirez's help. It was a complex task that I never would have believed my students could handle. To my surprise and delight, most did very well, and I knew they had really learned.

My professional development experience this year has changed the way I view what needs to be taught and learned, and I look forward to continuing to learn how to incorporate my new perspective further into my teaching.

Ideas for Future Professional Development

Based on the progress I made this year (see previous section), I believe I need to continue my efforts. I would like to continue to pursue the broad goal of improving my teaching and student learning on concepts and skills related to fractions, decimals, and percents. This would mean refining the unit I developed this year, including making some changes in the assessment. I am not yet confident in rubric development. With another opportunity to apply these things in my classes, I know my teaching will continue to improve.

Submitted by ___*Eileen Blanchard*___

Date ___*May 21, 2006*___

---

performance data, lesson plans demonstrating instructional interventions, and other similar documentation.

The Summative Review Conference

The summative review conference is a time for each teacher and supervisor to meet and review the teacher's progress in a more formal way. Unlike previous conferences focused on continuing growth and improvement, the summative conference takes stock of progress over time and offers written recommendations for future growth.

To maximize the opportunity for meaningful dialogue during this conference, supervisors should ask teachers to submit their final report of progress at least a few days before the conference date. This gives supervisors time to think about the narrative, list any questions they may have, and provide thoughtful feedback. Some additional suggestions for supervisors conducting summative review conferences include the following:

• Ask the teacher to lead the initial discussion of the final report of progress and artifacts. This recognizes that the teacher is the director of his or her own growth and development.

• Ask questions that help the teacher clarify and elaborate on ideas and understandings addressed in the final report.

• Guide the discussion toward the experiences that affected the teacher's perceptions and attitudes toward teaching and learning. Remember, one of the most effective ways to change attitudes is to change behavior (DuFour & Eaker, 1998).

• Engage the teacher in a discussion of two important issues: (1) that teachers need to know what "essential learning" is and how it is related to standards (TP-1); and (2) that we only know that students have learned something when they can perform a relatively complex task applying that new skill or knowledge without rehearsal (TP-2).

• Invite the teacher to elaborate on ideas for future professional development, and offer additional suggestions that will continue to appropriately stretch the teacher's instructional capacity.

• Be sure to allow time for the teacher to ask questions or note any other special achievements related to broad professional responsibilities.

• At the end of the conference, provide the teacher with an overall verbal assessment of his or her performance and suggestions for future growth. Some of these suggestions should be prepared ahead of the meeting, while others should respond to the teacher's comments during the discussion.

Two additional notes: the summative review meeting is not the time to raise concerns about the teacher's progress on the professional development plan or point out deficiencies in the teacher's final report of progress. These issues should be addressed prior to the meeting. In addition, thorough preparation is critical to the effectiveness of the summative conference, even if that requires rescheduling the conference.

The Supervisor's Summative Evaluation Report

After the summative evaluation conference, the supervisor develops the summative evaluation report to capture his or her perceptions of the teacher's overall performance, based on all that has been observed during the year, as well as the teacher's reflections on his or her work and growth. Once the report is complete, it is shared with the teacher and discussed in a brief follow-up meeting. This step ensures that the teacher understands what is stated in the evaluation and provides the teacher the opportunity to discuss any concerns about the evaluation's content or register differences of perspective. Figure 8.4 shows Gary's summative evaluation of Eileen Blanchard.

Several aspects of Gary's summative evaluation are noteworthy, both from the standpoint of effective supervision and evaluation and for what they tell us about Performance-Based Supervision and Evaluation:

• Note that Gary commends Eileen's general performance, extra effort, persistence, willingness to develop new units of instruction, and thorough preparation of her final report of progress. Commending effort and achievement as a form of positive feedback is central to further motivating and engaging adult learners (Bransford, Brown, & Cocking, 2000).

• The summative evaluation focuses most heavily on the teacher's progress on the improvement objective and the professional development plan. Gary's report emphasizes Eileen's study

Figure 8.4
Summative Evaluation Report on Eileen Blanchard

Annual Performance Evaluation
Fairview Public Schools

Staff Member: Eileen Blanchard   School Year: 2005–2006
Primary Instructional Assignment: 7th Grade Mathematics
Secondary Instructional Assignment: None
Primary Supervisor: Gary Mulholland, Principal

SECTION I. Supervisor Comments Regarding Overall Performance in the Instructional Assignment

Eileen Blanchard demonstrates satisfactory performance in all areas specified by the teacher's job description. Working in concert with her principal and district department chairperson, she has identified specific areas of teaching that she is committed to work on and improve. She developed and pursued a professional development plan that established a starting point for her work this year and that she will expand upon in the coming year (see Section II). The focus of Eileen's professional development plan is supportive of the school's strategic plan, as it is aimed at improving student performance in mathematics.

Eileen consistently works harmoniously and productively with colleagues, and extends her relationships with children through regular support of various student activities.

SECTION II. Supervisor Comments Regarding the Staff Member's Progress with the Professional Development Plan

Eileen based the focus of this year's plan on a preliminary analysis of state mastery test data that showed deficiencies in student performance in mathematics. She identified one area that has been a perennial problem (fractions, decimals, and percents) and determined to improve student proficiency in that area through work with students in her own classes. Early in the development of her plan to do so, and with the coaching of her supervisors, she realized that simply giving students more of the same instruction they had experienced would not make a significant difference. She understood that the mastery test was standards based and, as such, it tested students in their abilities to apply mathematics learning to complex problems. This is a skill that Eileen recognized that she had not really been teaching, nor was she confident in how to do it. Thus, Eileen defined two initial challenges:

1. To become knowledgeable about mathematics standards and how they relate to the mastery test and to the development of units of instruction.
2. To become proficient in developing units of instruction around mathematics standards, including the development of authentic performance-based assessments and rubrics.

(continued)

Figure 8.4   *(continued)*

Eileen came to realize, with reinforcement from her supervisors, that her mastery of the above two challenges was prerequisite to doing serious and extensive implementation of new approaches to teaching fractions, decimals, and percents in the classroom. Eileen made these the centerpieces of her professional development work during this year. Working continuously and collaboratively with her district department chairperson, she made notable progress, as evidenced by her demonstrated ability to

- Review, comprehend, and summarize literature describing mathematics standards.
- Demonstrate an emerging level of competence in designing a unit of study around standards and demonstrate like competence in developing a performance-based assessment.
- Demonstrate an emerging ability to construct rubrics for use with assessments.
- Implement a challenging, standards-based mathematics unit and related assessment that resulted in strong student achievement data.
- Show an improved ability to translate an analysis of student performance data into decisions about teaching.

Descriptions of these areas of progress and actual artifacts of evidence supporting them are included in Eileen's "Professional Development Plan: Final Report of Progress" (attached).

SECTION III. Commendations and Recommendations

Eileen Blanchard is commended for the positive attitude she brings to her work in general. The effort she makes to work productively with colleagues, coupled with her extended attention to students and their activities, make her an asset to the school. Eileen is especially commended for the persistence she brought to her work with her professional development plan this year, and for the improvement she made as described in this document.

It is recommended that Eileen extend her professional development focus next year by continuing to work more deeply on standards-based instruction and assessment in fractions, decimals, and percents. In addition, it is recommended that Eileen focus on improving her teaching performance in an area of essential learning in mathematics other than the one she focused on this year. In crafting her professional development plan for next year, Eileen will also need to base her work more specifically on showing the effects of improved teaching through student performance data. A carefully designed and specific performance objective that projects measurable increases in student learning will provide the basis for such a demonstration.

Teacher ___*Eileen Blanchard*_____   Date _*5/27/06*_

Primary Supervisor ___*Gary Mulholland*_____   Date _5/27/06_ of standards-based curriculum and authentic assessment, and then her development of a unit of study, related performance task, and assessment rubric. With each of these elements in place, it is Eileen's subsequent and rudimentary analysis of student performance data that begins to move her into the role of an action researcher.

• Gary's recommendations suggest that Eileen continue her work with standards-based instruction and performance assessment, but he encourages her to identify a second area of need related to math content knowledge and skills. This will reinforce her procedural understanding of the PBSE action research process and give Eileen a "fresh start" in the coming school year by prompting her to take another look at the state's 8th grade standardized math test and identify another area where student performance is low.

• Finally, Gary challenges Eileen to develop a specific student learning objective for the focus of her next professional development plan. During this first year of PBSE implementation, Eileen needed and took more time to increase her own understanding of "essential learning" and performance assessment. In Year Two, it's important that she become more focused in her work and concentrate on applying her new knowledge to instruction and assessment that improves student learning. Gary's challenge to Eileen reinforces the high expectations he holds for all Fairview faculty members and balances the more patient approach he and Charlie took with Eileen during Year One.

What About Marcia and Larry?

Just about everyone wants to know how a story ends. Let's take a look—albeit a more abbreviated one—at the experiences of our other Fairview teachers during the summative review process. Because Larry and Marcia each have a unique improvement objective and professional development plan, their paths evolve a bit differently.

◢ Prior to his end-of-year evaluation conference, Larry Rinaldi conducted one final assessment of his target students' progress to prepare for a longitudinal report of his students' fitness levels. As he had aimed for in his student learning objective, almost every student in his Fitness Club had moved up a level in each area of physical fitness, and all had used their journals to record both their efforts and their increasingly positive attitudes toward physical activity. Larry captured their performance data on the assessment sheet he had created, as he knew that this would be a central artifact for his final report of progress (see Figure 8.5).

After completing the chart, Larry reviewed the data and decided to measure the changes in student performance from the beginning of the year to the final assessment in June. He was interested in individual growth and how much growth the girls achieved collectively in each of the areas on his fitness assessments. Figure 8.6 (see p. 150) shows the results.

Larry's analysis demonstrated that although there was improvement in all four fitness areas, the one-mile run and push-ups continued to present the most challenge. Larry was pleased with the Fitness Club members' overall progress, but he wanted to continue working with these girls and possibly extend his improvement objective to the next school year, provided that the need was substantiated by data for the incoming 7th grade class.

Gary was impressed by Larry's verbal and written reflection. The PE teacher's ability to interpret and use student performance data to plan instruction had grown significantly, as had his skills in identifying standards-based interventions to meet specific student learning needs. In the principal's judgment, Larry's final report of progress, along with the many artifacts from his work throughout the year, confirmed that he had achieved competency in all the skills relative to the Teacher Preparation Phase of the Criteria of Excellence. In the coming year, Larry would focus more directly on the skills linked to indicators within the Initial Collaboration Phase.

At Marcia's summative review conference, she presented and explained her students' growth during the year and presented supporting evidence. One of the artifacts she shared was a form she had created for collecting student writing performance data over time (see Figure 8.7, p. 151).

Marcia's focus was to bring each of her targeted students into the "proficient" range. To do so would mean that each would have to earn a score of 4 or higher in both of the identified skills areas (Support and Detail, and Comprehensiveness). All but three students had achieved this level of performance, and all the targeted students had made progress. As Marcia shared the "before and after" work of individual members of her Period C class, she explained to Gary how reinforcing writing skills in her social studies class had benefited all her students—not just the targeted ones—and had also supported the work of her language arts colleague.

Figure 8.5
Longitudinal Fitness Club Assessment Data

Student Name	One-Mile Walk/Run			Sit and Reach			Right-Angle Push-Ups			Curl-Ups		
	Nov	Feb	Apr	June	Nov	Feb	Apr	June	Nov	Feb	Apr	June	Nov	Feb	Apr	June
Amanda	1	1	1	2	1	1	2	2	1	1	1	1	1	1	1	2
Courtney	2	2	2	3	2	3	3	4	2	2	2	3	2	2	2	3
Gabby	2	2	2	2	2	3	3	3	1	2	2	2	2	2	2	3
Irina	1	1	2	2	2	2	3	3	1	1	1	1	1	1	1	2
Keisha	1	1	1	1	1	2	2	3	1	1	1	2	1	2	2	2
Phoenix	2	2	2	2	2	2	2	3	1	2	2	2	2	2	2	3
Selena	2	2	2	2	2	2	3	3	1	1	1	2	2	2	2	2
Tamika	1	2	2	2	2	2	3	3	1	1	1	1	2	2	2	2
Wanda	1	1	1	1	1	2	2	2	1	1	1	1	1	1	1	2

Scale: 5 = Challenge Level; 4 = Health Level; 3 = Nearly Health Level; 2 = Below Health Level; 1 = Significantly Below Health Level

Figure 8.6
Numeric Analysis of Fitness Club Members' Progress

Student Name	Mile Walk/Run			Sit and Reach			Right-Angle Push-Ups			Curl-Ups		
	Nov	June	Levels Gained	Nov	June	Levels Gained	Nov	June	Levels Gained	Nov	June	Levels Gained
Amanda	1	2	1	1	2	1	1	1	0	1	2	1
Courtney	2	3	1	2	4	2	2	3	1	2	3	1
Gabby	2	2	0	2	3	1	1	2	1	2	3	1
Irina	1	2	1	2	3	1	1	1	0	1	2	1
Keisha	1	1	0	1	3	2	1	2	1	1	2	1
Phoenix	2	2	0	2	3	1	1	2	1	2	3	1
Selena	2	2	0	2	3	1	1	2	1	2	2	0
Tamika	1	2	1	2	3	1	1	1	0	2	2	0
Wanda	1	1	0	1	2	1	1	1	0	1	2	1
Average # Levels Gained			.44			1.22			.56			.78

Scale: 5 = Challenge Level; 4 = Health Level; 3 = Nearly Health Level; 2 = Below Health Level; 1 = Significantly Below Health Level

Figure 8.7
Targeted Students' Progress on Persuasive Writing Skills—May

Student Name	Support and Detail			Comprehensiveness		
	Oct	*Jan**	*May*	*Oct*	*Jan**	*May*
Maggie	3	4	5	3	4	4
George**	3	3	3	3	3	3
Miguel	2	3	4	3	3	4
Tanya	2	4	5	3	4	4
Zachary	2	3	4	3	3	4
Ethan	3	4	5	3	3	4
Matt	2	3	4	2	3	4
Jasmine**	3	3	3	3	3	3
Jim	2	3	4	3	4	5
Candace	3	4	4	3	3	4
Jose**	2	3	3	2	2	3

*Consensus score derived through discussion with the 8th grade language arts teacher.
**Students who fell short of the learning objective.
Note: Writing was scored on a rubric of 6 (Well-Developed) to 1 (Undeveloped);
4 = Proficient.

She and the 8th grade language arts teacher now used the same rubric to assess persuasive writing, ensuring that students would get a consistent message in both disciplines. Marcia's 8th graders were now better prepared to respond to the challenges of 9th grade writing assignments across the curriculum and better prepared for the state-mandated testing.

Marcia's work throughout the year, coupled with her demonstrated professional growth in the annual review meeting, left no doubt in Gary's mind that she had not only enhanced her own professional competence but contributed to the collective instructional capacity of the entire school. Nonetheless, Marcia's response to Gary's very positive feedback was one of dissatisfaction. She reminded Gary of her original student learning objective:

> By May 1 of this academic year, students in my Period C social studies class who scored in the Near Proficiency range (holistic score of 3.0–3.9) on the October writing sample will score in the Proficient or Exceeds Proficient range by demonstrating improvement in Support and Detail and Comprehensiveness in persuasive writing related to the social studies curriculum.

As her final summative assessment of student writing skills indicated, only 73 percent—or 8—of the Near Proficient students had achieved that goal. Marcia suggested that she evaluate the writing skills of next year's incoming 8th grade class, and if warranted, redouble her efforts to integrate quality writing instruction into her social studies classes. Her intended focus? Those students whose academic profile matched those of George, Jasmine, and Jose: this year's students whom she had "failed to get over the top." ◪

Both Larry Rinaldi and Marcia Williams offer portraits of teachers who have grown tremendously in their ability to ground instruction in essential, standards-based learning, and to use student performance data to inform instruction. Their unfailingly high expectations for student learning and their willingness to use assessment data to modify instruction demonstrate their ability to attend to the individual learning needs of students and contextualized instruction. And the energy that they bring to their own professional development is, in our experience, an authentic representation of the engaging power of the PBSE model.

Reality Check: Summative Evaluation and the Resistant or Deficient Teacher

Our discussion of summative evaluation would be incomplete without a few words about a difficult subject: what to do when a teacher is persistently resistant to participating in the PBSE model and how to work with a teacher who fails to make progress, despite supervisory support.

All supervisors must work hard to maintain the dignity of those with whom they work. Faculty members like Eileen Blanchard, who genuinely struggle with their new learning and with the PBSE process, deserve patience and support: time and resources will help them to make slow but steady progress. PBSE supervisors should be direct, specific, and concrete when working with the "Eileens" on a faculty, so that they are not allowed to flounder. In addition, embedding the PBSE model within a school culture makes it harder for teachers to fall through the cracks because it normalizes the process as "the way we do things around here."

Nonetheless, there may be the occasional teacher who is stubbornly resistant or does not make acceptable progress. Consider the following scenarios:

- A teacher who, like Eileen in the first year of the PBSE professional development plan, never really got into the action research process in any depth, but then made little additional progress in the second year. How long is too long to delay building teacher capacity to improve student learning?
- A teacher who did not make the minimal response that Eileen did in the first few months of her work and even avoided making contact with his or her supervisor at mid-cycle. How patient should the supervisor be?
- A teacher who is quietly struggling with the PBSE process but is embarrassed to admit this and attempts to hide this lack of confidence and instructional growth behind a flurry of other general initiatives and accomplishments, such as organizing assemblies, leading student activities, or recruiting school volunteers. Isn't instruction the priority?
- A teacher who believes that PBSE is simply another educational fad and chooses to respond to supervisory activities minimally, preferring instead to fall back on the old forms and processes for goal setting, observations, and conferencing. Is there room for passive resistance?

While each teacher's situation will be unique, there are several strategies that we have found to be helpful in working with resistant or deficient teachers. First, as in any effective program of teacher evaluation, a supervisor should not wait until the summative review to address problematic situations. Acknowledging that there is a problem and working openly to resolve it is both fair and proactive. Second, in order to plan an appropriate intervention, it is important to identify the cause of the problem: aptitude, effort, or other factors. This may best be accomplished through an open conversation with the teacher in which the supervisor attempts to determine what progress, if any, the teacher has made and what factors may be influencing a lack of sufficient progress. At that point, it is important to agree on a clear, concrete, and manageable number of tasks for the teacher to complete within an established time frame (we suggest three or four) and be prepared to discuss at the next scheduled meeting. The accountability for completing these tasks should be clear to the teacher and upheld by the supervisor.

When the process is reworked into a set of short-range initiatives, teachers who are struggling with the concept of PBSE typically demonstrate steadier progress. However, if the problem is deep-seated resistance, a lack of progress over the course of a year despite sustained intervention and support may force the supervisor to follow district protocol for working with a teacher who has not fulfilled expectations for professional responsibilities. When the professional culture of the school continues to grow, stubbornly resistant teachers will find that they no longer "fit in" among their colleagues and will sense the disconnect on a personal level as well on a professional one. As unfortunate as this is, the faculty and the school must move forward in their efforts to grow professionally and to help students to learn at challenging levels.

Summing Up the Summative Aspects of PBSE

The last several weeks of the academic year are a busy time for every educator. For the supervisor who is conducting summative review conferences and writing summative review reports among all the other end-of-year responsibilities, it can be difficult to muster additional time for professional reflection. For PBSE supervisors, a more thoughtful consideration of where teachers are collectively in their professional growth and how this intersects with building instructional capacity for school improvement may well extend into the weeks that follow the close of the school year (see Chapter 9). Nonetheless, our experience has shown that these supervisors will have already begun to see the beneficial effects of the PBSE model:

- They will have a picture of every teacher's growth and capacity and will be able to report this information at any given point in time.
- They will have a strong sense of how far the faculty as a whole has come, what each teacher needs to do next, and where they might secure the resources to undertake future professional development.
- They will have acquired a wealth of teacher-produced data: an unprecedented body of evidence about what is really happening in their school. This puts supervisors in a very favorable position when it is time to review their school improvement plan.

 KEYSTONE

Clinical supervision has made a considerable contribution to our growing body of professional knowledge by articulating and addressing a teacher's prerequisite instructional skills. However, it is far more a model of compliance than a resource for instructional capacity building. The action research orientation of PBSE represents the opportunity for each educator to stretch beyond, developing both a deep understanding of student learning and contextualized skills for teaching and assessment. Authority and accountability for professional growth shift to the teacher, engendering a sense of professional control and pride. The model also connects the teacher in meaningful ways with student progress, offering timely, standards-based performance data as opposed to the typically delayed data from standardized tests. As a result, the tangible effects that improved instruction has on student learning inspire change in both teacher action and teacher perception.

9

Developing Culture and Capacity in the Learning Community

We have discussed Performance-Based Supervision and Evaluation from the standpoint of individual educators and their unique experiences using student data to inform instruction in areas of essential learning. As the PBSE process unfolds, individual growth becomes interwoven among faculty members and results in stronger collective instructional capacity. This enhances the professional culture of the school.

The Criteria of Excellence can function as a tool for monitoring and demonstrating collective professional growth. The indicators found in each phase of the Criteria provide the means to show where teachers "are," developmentally speaking, at different points in time, and how the faculty as a whole has grown over time.

◢ Late in June, Gary Mulholland sat at a table in his office, surrounded by the files he used to organize the artifacts from his supervisory work with his staff members. The last school bus had rolled down the driveway at Fairview Middle School nearly two weeks earlier, teachers had already embarked on their summer activities, and Gary's own well-deserved vacation was just three weeks away. With the more managerial tasks associated with the close of the academic year behind him, Gary turned his full attention to the work he and his teachers had accomplished, particularly in their efforts with Performance-Based Supervision and Evaluation.

It had been a challenging and exciting year for everyone. In thinking about his end-of-year conversation with each teacher, Gary was both proud of and grateful for the sincere efforts his teachers had made, and his intuitive perception was that everyone had grown in their capacity to strategically address the specific learning needs of Fairview's students. Now it was time to conduct a data-based assessment: how had PBSE affected the overall instructional capacity of his staff and the culture of his school? The findings would inform Gary's work with staff in the coming year and provide direction for his own professional development.

To gather and organize data, Gary returned to the Criteria of Excellence, specifically to the indicators—the skills to be mastered and the tasks to be completed by each teacher and supervisor. Although the full array of Criteria of Excellence spanned six phases (see Appendix A), Gary decided to focus on just the first three—Teacher Preparation, Initial Collaboration, and Initial Monitoring—as most of his teachers' work had been concentrated there. He reviewed each teacher's file and made a thoughtful judgment about that teacher's end-of-year status relative to the Criteria indicators. Then, he organized the data into a tabular format (see Figure 9.1, p. 158).

Gary knew that to acquire a deep understanding of the change in his staff's overall capacity, he would need to consider the data he'd collected in different ways. First, he looked at the data for the Teacher Preparation Phase from the standpoint of teacher growth. He had already aggregated some data about staff members' skills and accomplishments in this phase, having gathered it during his initial conferences in the fall (see Figures 6.1 and 6.2). Now, he developed a spreadsheet that displayed the changes between his assessments at the beginning of the year and where he judged teachers to be at year's end and used this spreadsheet to generate a chart depicting the differences in the percent of teachers at each of the three levels of skill development (see Figure 9.2, p. 159).

The table and chart confirmed that many Fairview teachers had made dramatic gains in their ability to identify standards-based data and classroom performance data, organize the data and draw conclusions about their meaning, and begin to develop ideas about how to grow professionally in order to help students learn at more challenging levels. At the end of the year, there were certainly more teachers in the competent range on all of the indicators. Even so, not all staff members had developed full expertise with these skills and tasks. Gary noted that those who fell into the "emerging" or "just beginning" stages of development would need continuing support and specifically crafted professional development to address their needs. To target the most effective activities for these teachers, he would likely need to conduct another analysis of their skills at the start of the new school year so that he could factor in the learning needs of these teachers' incoming students. Gary's second challenge would be

Figure 9.1

Summary of Teachers' Skill-Level Status at the End of Year One of PBSE

Indicator	Focus of the Indicator	# Teachers per Skill Level and % of Total Faculty*		
		Competent	Emergent	Just Beginning
TP-1	Identifying standards-based student data	42 (91%)	3 (7%)	1 (2%)
TP-2	Identifying performance-based student data	40 (87%)	5 (11%)	1 (2%)
TP-3	Organizing data in multiple ways	31 (67%)	3 (7%)	12 (26%)
TP-4	Identifying data-based strengths and weaknesses	41 (89%)	4 (9%)	1 (2%)
TP-5	Drawing conclusions from data	32 (70%)	8 (17%)	6 (13%)
TP-6	Identifying artifacts of student work	40 (87%)	4 (9%)	2 (4%)
TP-7	Identifying ideas for modifying teaching	30 (65%)	6 (13%)	10 (22%)
IC-1	Reviewing data analysis and ideas for improvement	40 (87%)	5 (11%)	1 (2%)
IC-2	Extending initial data analysis	31 (67%)	5 (11%)	10 (22%)
IC-3	Generating ideas for a professional development plan	39 (85%)	7 (15%)	0 (0%)
IC-4	Generating ideas for building teacher capacity	30 (65%)	7 (15%)	9 (20%)
IC-5	Finalizing a teacher improvement objective	38 (83%)	7 (15%)	1 (2%)
IC-6	Developing a detailed action plan for PD	38 (83%)	7 (15%)	1 (2%)
IC-7	Supervisor and teacher agree to supervisory activities	N/A	N/A	N/A
IM-1	Implementing the improvement objective	39 (85%)	4 (9%)	3 (7%)
IM-2	Implementing the professional development plan	39 (85%)	6 (13%)	1 (2%)
IM-3	Maintaining appropriate communication	42 (91%)	3 (7%)	1 (2%)
IM-4	Supervisor monitors and facilitates the teachers efforts	N/A	N/A	N/A

*N = 46

Figure 9.2
Teacher Preparation Phase: Year One Longitudinal Changes in
Teachers' Skill-Level Status by Indicator

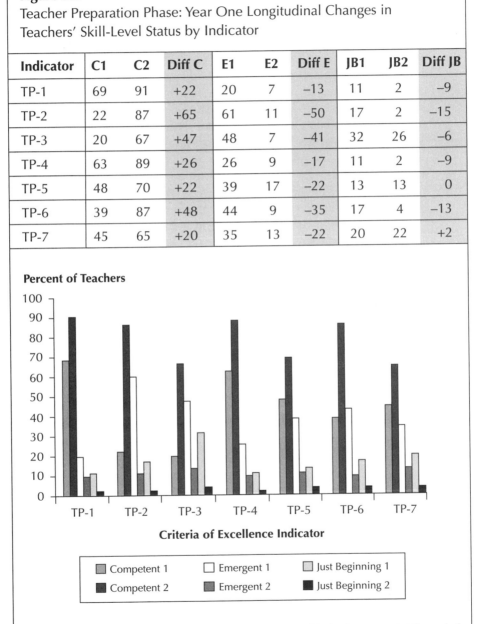

Indicator	C1	C2	Diff C	E1	E2	Diff E	JB1	JB2	Diff JB
TP-1	69	91	+22	20	7	−13	11	2	−9
TP-2	22	87	+65	61	11	−50	17	2	−15
TP-3	20	67	+47	48	7	−41	32	26	−6
TP-4	63	89	+26	26	9	−17	11	2	−9
TP-5	48	70	+22	39	17	−22	13	13	0
TP-6	39	87	+48	44	9	−35	17	4	−13
TP-7	45	65	+20	35	13	−22	20	22	+2

Percent of Teachers

Criteria of Excellence Indicator

Competent 1   Emergent 1   Just Beginning 1
Competent 2   Emergent 2   Just Beginning 2

C1 = % judged competent at the beginning of the year; C2 = % judged competent at the end of
the year; Diff C = Difference between C1 and C2; E1 = % judged emergent at the beginning of
the year; E2 = % judged emergent at the end of the year; Diff E = Difference between E1 and
E2; JB1 = % judged just beginning at the beginning of the year; JB2 = % judged just beginning
at the end of the year; Diff JB = difference between JB1 and JB2.

to provide those staff members who had achieved competence in this phase's skills with continuing opportunities for professional growth.

Gary knew he should take his analysis to a deeper level and try to connect what the data had revealed to specific capacity-building initiatives, but he wasn't sure how to do that. He decided to call a district colleague, elementary school principal Diana Fernandez, for advice. Diana was implementing PBSE at her own school and was more than happy to help. Over the course of an afternoon meeting, they decided to frame Gary's analysis of teacher growth from the standpoints of collective strengths and collective weaknesses (or "areas for future effort"). Both agreed they should set the standard for PBSE skill mastery quite high, determining that a Criteria of Excellence indicator would be deemed "mastered" in a collective sense if 80 percent of faculty members were judged to have achieved competency in it. Conversely, if 20 percent or more of the teachers were still at the "just beginning" stage of development, that indicator would be a focus for additional attention in the coming year.

Returning to Gary's first data table (see Figure 9.1), the two principals noted that indicators IC-5, IC-6, and IC-7 within the Initial Collaboration Phase and all the indicators within the Initial Monitoring Phase (IM-1 through IM-4) represented procedural activities rather than skills. Accordingly, they decided to apply the standards for mastery only to the Teacher Preparation Phase and the first four indicators of the Initial Collaboration Phase (see Figure 9.3).

Viewing the indicators in this way helped Gary to see that the areas that his staff members had mastered were fairly basic: the skills a teacher needed to begin to use a PBSE approach to set an improvement objective and create a professional development plan. Nonetheless, they represented the faculty's growing collective capacity, and Gary knew that teachers who were "competent" on these indicators would be important resources for colleagues who still needed support. With such a broad mastery of these skills across the faculty, it would be easy to arrange for peer assistance on PBSE within a content discipline or grade level.

Gary used a similar process to identify the collective areas of weakness: those indicators on which 20 percent or more of his teachers were at a "just beginning" stage of development (see Figure 9.4). As he began to array the data, however, he noticed that Indicator TP-5 ("the teacher draws conclusions from data"), with a combined 30 percent of the faculty at the "just beginning" or "emergent" level, also showed a need for support. He decided to include this skill as a focus for PBSE implementation efforts in the coming year.

When Gary reviewed the areas that would be the targets for future improvement efforts, he noted that they represented complex skills: the ability to look at data from different perspectives, to extend data analysis, to draw conclusions from multiple data sources, and to derive relevant

Figure 9.3
Indicators at Mastery Level by the End of Year One
of PBSE Implementation

Indicator	Focus of the Indicator	# Teachers per Skill Level and % of Total Faculty*		
		Competent	*Emergent*	*Just Beginning*
TP-1	Identifying standards-based student data	42 (91%)	3 (7%)	1 (2%)
TP-2	Identifying performance-based student data	40 (87%)	5 (11%)	1 (2%)
TP-4	Identifying data-based strengths and weaknesses	41 (89%)	4 (9%)	1 (2%)
TP-6	Identifying artifacts of student work	40 (87%)	4 (9%)	2 (4%)
IC-1	Reviewing data analysis and ideas for improvement	40 (87%)	5 (11%)	1 (2%)
IC-3	Generating ideas for a professional development plan	39 (85%)	7 (15%)	0 (0%)

*N = 46

Figure 9.4
Targeted Indicators for Year Two of PBSE Implementation

Indicator	Focus of the Indicator	# Teachers per Skill Level and % of Total Faculty*		
		Competent	*Emergent*	*Just Beginning*
TP-3	Organizing data in multiple ways	31 (67%)	3 (7%)	12 (26%)
TP-5	Drawing conclusions from data	32 (70%)	8 (17%)	6 (13%)
TP-7	Identifying ideas for modifying teaching	30 (65%)	6 (13%)	10 (22%)
IC-2	Extending initial data analysis	31 (67%)	5 (11%)	10 (22%)
IC-4	Generating ideas for building teacher capacity	30 (65%)	7 (15%)	9 (20%)

*N = 46

ideas for planning teacher learning. Not surprisingly, there were teachers who had made great advances in these areas during the year, and yet still struggled to look at data deeply and craft professional development plans to enhance student learning. As expected, these teachers would need continuing support in their second year's work within the PBSE model. Close work with them would be an important part of Gary's future supervisory responsibilities. ◪

Using Data on Teacher Growth to Improve Capacity and Culture

Conducting data analysis to strategically inform planning and practice is just as important for school administrators as it is for individual faculty members. Nonetheless, translating data into real action remains a significant challenge. To effect school improvement by building collective instructional capacity, school leaders themselves must be able to identify relevant data sources, examine this information from multiple perspectives, and determine what the data mean for future efforts.

As the example of Gary Mulholland shows, this is a complex undertaking. Individual faculty members will be at different stages of skill mastery, meaning they will require personalized professional development. Some PBSE skills are harder to master than others, requiring more time and more support. The data may also be "messy" (as in the example of the TP-5 indicator that did not quite meet the 20-percent-or-higher standard) and demand individual consideration. Nonetheless, we see that a supervisor like Gary—by first taking the time to reflect on his own experiences and those of his faculty and then collecting and analyzing data relative to their accomplishments—can bring the PBSE model full circle to prepare for the work to be done in the new academic year.

Information on the collective knowledge and skills for an entire faculty offers a broad picture of where teachers are in their professional growth. This allows a supervisor like Gary to plan for future work with groups of teachers who have common learning needs and to seek out professional development relevant to those needs.

It also reveals which teachers have developed particular expertise with specific skills. These teachers can be invaluable resources for colleagues in their own school or even across the school district.

The Criteria of Excellence as a Cycle of Learning

The Criteria of Excellence represent a cyclic approach to building individual and collective instructional capacity. As such, a teacher's progress through the phases can be adjusted to his or her growth needs. Sometimes the journey lasts a year and a half or more, and sometimes it will loop back to earlier indicators within the process until the individual's skills are developed to a level that the supervisor deems competent. When the teacher is ready to bring closure to the learning cycle, both the teacher and the supervisor can do so, reflect, and prepare for the next cycle of professional growth. In addition, the indicators associated with each phase of the Criteria of Excellence offer both teachers and supervisors a robust instrument for intersecting student performance data, content and performance standards, multiple assessment strategies, and professional development initiatives, all coalescing around an area of student need related to essential learning. Further, the Criteria continue to serve as a powerful tool at a number of levels and for different purposes within a teacher's cycle of learning. As noted in earlier chapters, these include the following:

• *Planning for the work of supervision and evaluation with individual teachers.* Throughout a cycle of professional growth, the Criteria of Excellence indicators help both the teacher and supervisor develop specific skills related to comprehensive data analysis, standards-based essential learning, and relevant professional development to address student learning needs. Reference to these indicators helps educators turn numbers, such as standardized and classroom assessment data, into action by connecting professional development to student learning.

• *Planning for supervision and evaluation with an array of educators.* Marcia, Eileen, and Larry offer portraits of teachers working in traditional content areas: social studies, mathematics, and physical education, respectively. PBSE works just as effectively with and for teachers whose professional responsibilities are ancillary to the traditional classroom: guidance counselors, school psychologists, and other support personnel. Because their professional development objectives are based on data, and because these educators support students in ways that increase learning and motivation to learn, their participation in the PBSE cycle of learning results in increased capacity to improve student learning—just as it does for classroom teachers.

• *Planning for the professional development needs of the entire faculty.* At times, it will be necessary to provide professional development experiences that address needs common to most if not all faculty members. We showed how, at Fairview Middle School, beginning the work of PBSE requires faculty members like Eileen and Larry to acquire additional professional skills in data analysis and the development of performance-based assessments. Principal Gary Mulholland appropriately arranges for year-long, sustained professional development in both areas through regular after-school seminars. After the first year of implementing PBSE, collective data on faculty needs will help Gary plan the most appropriate buildingwide professional development for teachers entering a second cycle of learning.

• *Use as a monitoring tool by individual teachers to guide their professional initiatives and measure their progress.* Supervisors are not the only ones who can use the indicators found within the Criteria of Excellence. As a form of self-assessment and self-monitoring, the indicators can help teachers keep themselves on target with the PBSE process and help them identify areas for further professional development. Our educators Marcia and Larry kept the Criteria close at hand to guide their work throughout their learning cycle.

-------------------------------- ▽ KEYSTONE --------------------------------

The power of the PBSE model resides in its ability to increase individual and collective teacher capacity, interconnect faculty members to support each other's learning, and provide a data-based roadmap for future professional development.

A Few Words on Team Initiatives

Throughout this book, we have emphasized the need for teachers and supervisors to collaborate in their efforts to improve teacher capacity for increasing student learning. We have also discussed how teachers might collaborate on certain professional development initiatives in order to support common learning needs and each other's growth.

Based on our experience as administrators, we can recommend another effective tool to support longitudinal teacher growth: team-level data analysis, planning, monitoring, and assessment. When teachers are asked what they need to help them meet their students' needs and achieve their own professional desires, they almost always mention "more time to talk with one another." Although we support common planning time at all levels of schooling, it's been our experience that this can be an ineffective use of the teachers' precious time unless there is a real focus for the conversation. Data can provide this focus. Every educator knows how team meeting time can evaporate due to the very real human need to vent frustrations or commiserate with those who do. And without specific student achievement information or samples of student work, it is difficult to provide colleagues with anything beyond moral support. Individual student work, along with aggregated and disaggregated datasets of student performance, provide an anchor for conversation and raise the discussion from an anecdotal (and perhaps emotional) conversation to a common point of practice measured by reasoned, articulated measures of achievement. When teams of teachers discuss real student performance data, they are less likely to prescribe what a given *member* of the team might do to improve learning and more apt to tackle the challenge *as a team,* deciding what needs to happen as indicated by the data.

Monitoring the Learning Community's Growth in Capacity and Culture

How will supervisors and teachers know when their efforts with PBSE have resulted in increased institutional capacity and a richer school culture? We recommend using multiple measures of progress to monitor a school's growth over time.

Collective Professional Growth

The Criteria of Excellence serve as both a common process and a common standard for measuring collective professional growth. Regularly aggregating faculty data for indicators within the Criteria of Excellence, as in Figure 9.1, offers a holistic picture of the teachers' collective skills. Pre- and post-assessment data comparisons, like the one in Figure 9.2, demonstrate clear and compelling evidence of professional growth over time.

Improvement in Student Learning

From a longitudinal perspective, improved student performance data, both standardized data and scores resulting from high-quality performance assessments, are effective indicators of a school's evolution toward becoming a true learning community. Due to the PBSE model's integration of teacher learning, strategic instruction, and analysis of student work, using student performance data as a key indicator is a fair and relevant component of the monitoring process.

Organizational Growth

By "organizational growth," we mean a school's quest to grow as a learning community. It is no accident that the attributes of Performance-Based Supervision and Evaluation are entirely consistent with Peter Senge's notion of the "learning organization" (1990). Senge identifies five attributes, or "disciplines," that provide an administrator with valuable ways to monitor a school's growth as a learning community. Let's take a look of how each dovetails with the PBSE model.

1. *Systems thinking.* This characteristic of a learning organization asserts that every school is a complex whole made up of many parts that interact and affect each other. Being able to see the subtle influence each part has on the others is a necessary prerequisite to developing the capacity for addressing complex, deeply rooted challenges. In PBSE, data are regularly used to inform decisions, both internal and external resources for professional development are valued, and teachers and supervisors collaborate to refine professional initiatives. The extent to which faculty is coming to understand itself as a system is a measure of its growth as a learning community.

2. *Personal mastery.* In Senge's model, personal mastery indicates a high level of proficiency in a particular field or skill, an attribute that invokes respect and results in strong and particularly effective outcomes. It requires that individuals commit themselves to lifelong learning as a continuous process. As teacher-learners, staff members use the PBSE process to guide their professional development—not only to achieve focused and continual growth, but also to model lifelong learning for their students. Growth in personal mastery is a sign of growth in school capacity.

3. *Mental models.* Senge's mental models represent images and paradigms: how an organization "pictures" itself and its various components. These conceptions of "who we are" and "how we do things" can powerfully affect a school's capacity for change, as deeply held mental models can suppress the school's ability to

grow. In PBSE, growth as a learning community is seen in the evolution of how faculty members picture their work and their role within the school. The extent to which mental models evolve and suggest innovative practices is a measure of increasing capacity.

4. *Building shared vision.* For Senge, shared vision is genuine. Members of the organization mutually determine how they picture the future, and their involvement in creating this vision motivates them to contribute sustained personal leadership in achieving that vision. Schools that elect to implement Performance-Based Supervision and Evaluation have already demonstrated a commitment to a different way of approaching practice. In addition, the positive student performance outcomes that result from strategic professional development and instructional intervention reinforce and enhance a common vision for involved faculty—another measure of increased school capacity.

5. *Team building.* This attribute of the learning organization distinguishes individual learning from the more collective, interactive, and dialogic learning that occurs within a team. Team building and collective team learning are critical to the growth of an organization. This aspect of Senge's model is foundational to Performance-Based Supervision and Evaluation, wherein the "team" may be a teacher and supervisor, a teacher and more-expert peer, a group of teachers, the entire faculty, or any number of other interactive assemblies. A unique feature of PBSE is that the roles of "teacher" and "learner" in professional development are highly contextualized, changing as the learning needs of each faculty member evolve and educators share their growing expertise with each other.

Enhanced School Culture

Beyond Senge's five indicators, supervisors and their faculties will want to return to one more effective signal of increasing capacity and enriched school culture: what Fullan (2001) refers to as the "reculturing" of the teaching profession. To achieve change in the teaching profession, Fullan advocates establishing a school culture in which teachers are respected and challenged, are encouraged to take a leadership role in improvement efforts, and have both autonomy and accountability; and in which a passion for learning and extensive collaboration are highly valued. These attributes can serve both as a vision and as a powerful rubric for measuring a school's progress toward becoming a true learning community.

What does a school look and sound like when it is a true learning community?

• The more formal teacher meetings, such as team meetings, faculty meetings, and professional development sessions, are increasingly focused on data, especially data related to student learning. These might include assessment results, student work samples, or instructional planning by the teacher.

• Informal "teacher talk" changes. When teachers begin to talk with each other before or after school, even at lunchtime, and they are talking about teaching and learning in ways that demonstrate deeper understanding and enthusiasm for their work, a cultural shift is taking place.

• Teachers' deepening understanding of teaching and learning permeates all aspects of their work, not just classroom instruction. In parent conferences, special education meetings, and any other meeting to discuss student progress, conversations look at students from a strength perspective and seek to move past barriers to learning.

• Conditions don't become causes. Instead of giving up on students because of insurmountable challenges, teachers seek to change conditions in order to find a different route to success (Cook, 2000).

• Within the district, among parents, and in the community, the work done by PBSE teachers and school leaders gains increasing credibility.

Communicating Professional Growth

Gains in organizational capacity and culture are evident in artifacts that portray improvements in student learning and the collective accomplishments of faculty. Requirements for principals to generate reports of progress to district leaders or the community are relatively commonplace. Within the PBSE model, the focus and content of these reports are much different.

◪ Having completed his data analysis for the first year of Performance-Based Supervision and Evaluation, Gary Mulholland prepared to write an end-of-year report of progress for his superintendent and the board of education. His previous annual reports of progress had detailed teacher and administrator activities; they were a summary of what had been *done* throughout the year. This year's report would focus on *outcomes,* with data presented in multiple formats to clearly convey the progress the faculty had made in their journey toward using PBSE to improve instruction and assessment and thus improve student learning. To portray these accomplishments in more depth, Gary interwove short vignettes of improved student learning throughout the report, along with examples of his faculty's individual and group learning experiences. ◪

A Continuing Commitment as a Learning Community

In the real world of practice, there is no single or even collective solution to building the institutional capacity and deepening the culture of each school. Even with the strategic, interconnected approach developed through supervision for learning and the Performance-Based Supervision and Evaluation model, growing enriched culture and capacity is a classroom-by-classroom, school-by-school endeavor. Making this happen means that our actions must be informed by a shared vision and an unwavering commitment to becoming a true learning community.

10

Applying the Model to Administrators

Although there is an abundance of professional literature addressing the supervision and evaluation of teachers, the literature focused on the supervision and evaluation of school administrators is comparatively scarce and offers far fewer recommendations for the development of school leaders. As Ginsberg and Berry (1990) put it, "the process of principal evaluation [has been] minimally studied and minimally changed over the years" (p. 112). What we do know, from the research available and from our own experience, is that the evaluation of principals often falls to immediate supervisors, who may be removed from and only marginally familiar with the principal's workplace. As a result, the performance feedback principals receive is typically superficial and has little effect on their ability to grow professionally or to further teachers' instructional development (Peterson, 2000; Weller, Buttery, & Bland, 1994).

Fortunately, a steady movement has begun that advocates linking administrator growth and evaluation to school improvement efforts. This approach offers school leaders substantially more support in their efforts to improve their own practice and that of their teachers. Performance-Based Supervision and Evaluation espouses this movement. It provides district-level administrators with the means to significantly strengthen the professional development of principals and other administrators, and thus boost the collective efficacy of an entire school district.

Administrator Evaluation for School Improvement

The evaluation of school administrators has traditionally been approached as a task unrelated to school improvement and, in some cases, unrelated to any other broad school or district initiative. The typical evaluation cycle for administrators follows a pattern similar to what teachers experience: a performance goal (or goals) set by the administrator and a superior at the beginning of the year; a mid-year meeting to review progress; and an end-of-year conference and the supervisor's final "write-up," in the form of a competency checklist, a narrative discussion of the administrator's progress on the goal and his or her work in general, or any one of a number of permutations of these formats. As the superiors rarely work in the same building as the administrator, actual observation of the administrator's work varies greatly; typically, the primary evidence is the administrator's own report of what has been accomplished. Data-based discussion is rare, and data-based discussion linked to standards of school leadership, even rarer. All told, this kind of administrator evaluation is unlikely to be strategic (purposeful in its selection of the most relevant and effective performance goal, based on identification of needs in areas of essential learning) or contextualized (responsive to the unique characteristics of the administrator's setting). It is no wonder that the limited study of administrator evaluation concludes that the more traditional models for this effort have had little effectiveness on administrators' growth.

As noted, the current climate of accountability for improved student performance has led to new forms of administrator evaluation more closely linked with school improvement planning, professional development, and teacher evaluation. The goal is to connect, align, and integrate these substantive areas of an administrator's work and thus, enhance his or her ability to increase the school's capacity to improve student learning. We have certainly seen this shift in our home state of Connecticut, where guidelines for school leader evaluation and professional development suggest that school leaders be assessed on how effectively they have responded to three critical job responsibilities:

1. Increasing student learning through a school improvement plan that focuses on enhancing teaching and learning.

2. Providing instructional leadership to teachers and students.

3. Acquiring strategic professional development relevant to their job responsibilities (Connecticut State Department of Education, 2002).

These guidelines openly assume that teacher and administrator competence directly affect student learning, that the instructional capacity of both school leaders and teachers is enhanced through professional development, and that professional development must be driven by the gap between high expectations for student achievement and actual student performance. The work that lies ahead demands a move away from disconnected professional initiatives and toward full integration of teacher evaluation, administrator evaluation, school improvement planning, and professional development—a true "systems thinking" approach (Senge, 1990).

How can educators achieve this integration? Acknowledging that each school district needs to develop its own mutually determined process that is sensitive to community context and district culture, priorities, and needs, there are several general strategies that educators can employ to promote integration of their professional work.

1. *Examine the effects of professional work, rather than the inputs.* This means making student work and other artifacts of accomplishment the center of professional dialogues, even those between a building-level administrator and his or her superior. It's

not enough to focus on the process of teaching or school leadership; the outcomes are really what matter most.

2. *Identify a professional vocabulary and use it consistently to promote clear communication and a common vision for teaching and learning.* The conversation begins with agreement on what constitutes strong teaching and learning, and is furthered by agreement on what type of supervision will support this vision.

3. *Continually develop skills in data collection, data analysis, and data interpretation.* Strong skills in this area allow teachers and administrators to look at their work more analytically, objectively, and deeply, and to provide guidance to colleagues who are just beginning to develop these skills.

4. *Use strategic planning and intervention to improve student learning.* Here is where school improvement and professional development intersect. Educators must identify the most appropriate professional intervention based on student learning needs, and then seek out the professional development experiences that will best assist them in implementing and refining that intervention.

5. *Reflect.* Thinking about practice and considering ways in which past experiences can inform future practice is critical to deepening understanding of teaching and learning.

Asserting that school improvement, teacher and administrator evaluation, and related professional development are critical to student learning may sound like an obvious understatement, but sadly, this alignment is far more common in recommendations and guidelines than it is in actual practice. Nonetheless, interfacing these four areas makes powerful sense and places student learning at the heart of all that happens in a school. Teachers and administrators need to grow in ways that make them more capable of addressing student learning needs, and they must be able to identify those needs through an examination of student performance data related to essential knowledge and skills. When this happens, everyone in the school is working toward a common goal: a vision of every student learning high-quality curriculum at a challenging level.

─────────────── ⬖ KEYSTONE ───────────────

Integration of teacher evaluation, administrator evaluation, school improvement planning, and professional development creates a continuous learning model for increasing the capacity of all members of the learning community to grow in knowledge, skills, dispositions, and professional efficacy.

Performance-Based Supervision and Evaluation of Administrators

If the preceding discussion sounds familiar, it should. These more recent trends in administrator evaluation reflect the key features of the Performance-Based Supervision and Evaluation that we have presented so far. Applied at the administrative level, PBSE provides a way to increase the culture and capacity of the school district as a whole. In addition, when school administrators participate in the same process that they ask of staff members, the credibility of their professional relationships grows, further developing the school and district as a community of continuous learners.

The process of implementing PBSE at the administrative level unfolds in much the same way as it does for teachers:

• *Identify an area of focus.* This should be a "slice" of essential learning for the administrator—one related to some element of the standards for school leadership set or followed by the district.

• *Use data to zero-in on a specific growth objective.* These data should come from both from standardized sources and from local assessments that confirm the area of need.

• *Align the focus with district priorities.* This ensures a strong link between the administrator's improvement objective and the school and district improvement plans.

• *Create a professional development plan.* Here, the administrator outlines what steps he or she will take to "get smarter" about developing the instructional capacity of faculty members, specifically in the focus area.

• *Continue to use data to monitor growth on the improvement objective.* Systematic data collection and analysis guide the administrator's accomplishment of his growth objective and may signal needed revision to the professional development plan.

• *Collect artifacts.* These artifacts serve as evidence of the administrator's work on the improvement objective.

• *Engage in ongoing reflection.* This helps to deepen understanding of standards-based curriculum, instruction, and assessment and identify further needs.

• *Engage in clear, specific, and data-rich communication between the administrator and the superior regarding progress on the improvement objective.* Our example principal, Gary Mulholland, has already experienced a change in his own communication with the superintendent: he can now specifically describe the instructional capacity of both individual teachers and the faculty as a whole.

As it does with teachers, PBSE underscores the professionalism of administrators. They take the lead in identifying the area of growth and relevant professional development. They experience both autonomy and accountability for their work. They are deeply engaged in their learning and find these efforts meaningful and authentic within the context of their job responsibilities. They connect with colleagues and external experts to support their own development, and they collaborate with others to lend expertise back. They are reenergized by the evolution of a new paradigm for their work and their growing competence in leadership for teaching and learning.

They can truly become the "lead learner" (Barth, 2001). Another visit with our friend Gary Mulholland illustrates how this happens.

◪ More than a year and a half ago, when the superintendent of Fairview Public Schools first proposed that administrators investigate Performance-Based Supervision and Evaluation, Gary and his administrative colleagues had attended a session on PBSE at a statewide conference. A few months later, the superintendent and all the district administrators participated in more extensive staff development led by PBSE consultants. Buoyed by the promise that this model seemed to hold, Gary and his colleague principals went on to work closely with teacher leaders in their schools to gain support for implementing the model.

There had certainly been some challenges during that first year of implementation, but there had been many successes as well: enough to prompt the sense among both teachers and administrators that the district's professional culture was already beginning to shift. Throughout the year, the new supervision and evaluation model was a regular agenda item at Administrative Council meetings. The superintendent, principals, directors, and district department chairpersons shared what was happening in their work with staff members, brainstormed ideas for professional development resources, and devised solutions to more complex challenges. The exchanges were substantively different from the more managerial conversations characteristic of previous Council meetings. Halfway through Year One, about the time when the administrators were scheduling their own mid-year supervisory conferences with their superiors, falling back on the old administrator evaluation model was already beginning to feel dissonant from their work with staff.

During the February Administrative Council meeting, one of the elementary school principals, Diana Fernandez, brought up what a number of her colleagues were already thinking. "We've been through substantial professional development with PBSE, we're implementing it with staff in our schools, and we talk about the model at every Council meeting. Yet last month, when we had our own mid-year evaluation meetings, we used the old reporting forms and the old process. We're already collecting data with our staff and trying to prioritize our efforts. Wouldn't it make more sense to use a PBSE approach with our own evaluation process?"

The question met with several nods of agreement. Certainly, the superintendent was encouraged to see this grassroots support for extending the implementation to the administrative level, and he commended the administrators for wanting to "practice what they preached." It was agreed that for the duration of that first year, PBSE would be used at the faculty level, but in July, the administrators would approach the development of their new improvement objectives by using the PBSE process, beginning with the four tests.

And so it was that Gary Mulholland found himself at the table in his office in late June, surrounded by the files he used to organize his PBSE work with teachers. He reviewed each teacher's PBSE file, aggregated the data regarding their progress on the Criteria of Excellence (see Figures 9.1 and 9.2), and reviewed the needs of his staff. Analysis and interpretation of student performance data and linking student achievement needs to relevant professional development continued to be areas for growth, both for teachers who were just beginning to use the PBSE process and for those who were farther along in their implementation of its strategies.

Gary recalled that James Feldman, the principal of the district's other middle school, had mentioned that his teachers would also need further support in these areas. He decided to give James a call to see if they might collaborate on mutual professional development in the coming year. By working together, they might even provide a more cohesive response to their teachers' learning needs. Gary also decided to approach the superintendent and have an initial conversation about using this work as his own improvement objective for the new academic year. After all, he would need to get smarter about data analysis and instructional intervention in order to fulfill a key administrative responsibility: effectively supporting the professional growth of his entire teaching staff. To that end, Gary drafted a parallel professional development plan for his own growth and supervisory responsibilities with Fairview Middle School teachers, based on faculty data analysis (see Figure 10.1).

Gary met with the superintendent during the second week in July to review the progress his teachers had made in PBSE implementation. He was especially proud of their improvement objectives and related professional development initiatives. He also brought along several artifacts from his summative review conferences with staff, including data analysis reports, professional development plans based on student needs in areas of essential learning, and reports of progress with these efforts. Gary also shared his own draft professional development plan for the coming year. Having a year's worth of experience with this model of supervision and evaluation, and having completed at least initial analysis of data on teacher performance, he had a much clearer and more strategic idea of how to plan for improving the learning of both his students and his faculty members.

Both Gary and the superintendent commented on how different this year's supervisory conference was from those they had shared in the past. Now, data provided the foundation for discussion of progress, they shared a deeper understanding of the professional growth Gary's teachers had achieved, and plans for future effort flowed logically from prior work. Even more important, Gary was able to clearly connect his efforts to build teacher instructional capacity to his school improvement plan's focus on high expectations for student learning. As they concluded the meeting,

Figure 10.1
Gary Mulholland's Draft Professional Development Plan

Plan for the Faculty	Time Line	Plan for the Administrator
	by September 30	• Investigate professional development resources for data analysis: research available in the literature and from the state department of education and regional educational services providers. • Meet with teachers regarding further professional development on data analysis to determine individual and collective needs.
	by October 15	• Meet with colleague James Feldman to plan inservice seminars on data analysis to be offered for teachers at both district middle schools. Sessions will be offered on the second and fourth Tuesday of each month, with new information presented at the first monthly session and peer discussion groups focused on applying new learning at the second monthly session. • Identify internal and external experts to lead the first seminar of each month.
• Professional development seminars open to all faculty members, but particularly encouraged for teachers at the "just beginning" level of skill development on TP-3, TP-5, and TP-7; or IC-2 and IC-4. • These seminars will occur twice a month from November through April.	by November 1 and 15	• Implement and participate in both November sessions: – Session 1: Introduction to Data Analysis – Session 2: Peer Discussion of the Initial Use of Data Analysis • Select focus for personal data analysis activities, using the four tests.
• Teacher participation and application of new learning in regard to organizing data in multiple formats.	by December 1 and 15	• Implement and participate in both December sessions: – Session 3: Organizing Data in Multiple Formats – Session 4: Peer Discussion of Organizing Data in Multiple Formats • Develop three different formats for looking at selected student achievement data.

(continued)

Figure 10.1   (*continued*)

Plan for the Faculty	Time Line	Plan for the Administrator
• Teacher participation and application of new learning regarding extending data analysis.	by January 2 and 15	• Implement and participate in both January sessions: – Session 5: Extending Data Analysis for Deeper Examination – Session 6: Peer Discussion of Extending Data Analysis • Extend the analysis of selected student achievement data through further disaggregation.
• Teacher participation and application of new learning related to drawing conclusions from data analysis.	by February 1 and 15	• Implement and participate in both February sessions: – Session 7: Drawing Conclusions from the Analysis of Data – Session 8: Peer Discussion of Drawing Conclusions from Data Analysis • Develop grounded and useful conclusions from the deep analysis of selected student achievement data.
• Teacher participation and application of new learning regarding developing initiatives to inform instructional practice.	by March 1 and 15	• Implement and participate in both March sessions: – Session 9: Developing Initiatives for Improving Practice – Session 10: Peer Discussion of Using Data to Inform Instructional Practice • Develop initiatives to improve student learning within the context of the school improvement plan.
• Due: Teachers' final report of progress, including summary of progress on improvement objective, artifacts, reflection on growth, and ideas for further learning.	by April 1	• Gather and organize draft individual and collective plans for teachers' further professional development. • Collect and organize teachers' final reports of progress and artifacts from teacher data analysis. • Collect and organize artifacts of own learning and that of the teachers participating in the seminars. • Develop written reflection on faculty and own growth during this learning cycle. • Draft ideas for teacher growth and own learning for the next PBSE cycle.

the superintendent wondered to himself if this approach might not be useful for his own work with the Fairview Board of Education. . . . ◢

When Gary Mulholland and his colleague administrators use data to inform their work as supervisors, they model the PBSE process for faculty. They also approach one of the most important aspects of their job responsibilities—working to develop the instructional capacity of their teachers—in a more knowledgeable and considered way: through continuous learning.

To further connect teacher development to student learning, principals like Gary, Diana, and James will also want to collect, analyze, and monitor student performance data from both standardized tests and high-quality local assessments. Is it dubious, controversial, or empirically invalid to make that connection? We don't think so. In Performance-Based Supervision and Evaluation, teachers' professional development and evaluation are predicated on identifying student learning needs relative to essential standards-based knowledge and skills. This connects teaching and learning in ways that are concrete, not inferential.

Traditionally, administrators asked to demonstrate evidence of student achievement have relied upon standardized test scores as an objective indicator of "how well the school was doing." Performance-Based Supervision and Evaluation offers a way to provide rich internal data. Content and performance standards frame the curriculum, assessments are standards based, and teacher development derives from student learning needs. As a result, local assessment data, as well as data that verify the growing instructional capacity of faculty members, are all valid indicators of how well the school is meeting student learning needs.

A Plea for Embracing Feedback

Administrators, just like teachers, improve more when they receive knowledgeable, timely, and relevant feedback about their practice. Yet too often, busy schedules and multiple responsibilities curb the amount of time and attention given to feedback, either for or by supervisors. A performance-based approach to practice is just that: focused on what the educator is doing to build capacity to meet student learning needs. Feedback informs that performance and once again offers a "systems" approach to continuing growth (Senge, 1990).

An administrator interested in deep professional growth will want to seek feedback from multiple sources (Oliva & Pawlas, 2004). Certainly, an administrator's own superior is a vital source of guidance. Within a school culture that values and respects feedback, teachers can also play an important role in offering commentary about and recommendations for the administrator's work. In addition, inviting teachers to contribute evaluative feedback represents a call for teachers to invite student feedback about their own work. Finally, self-assessment should be a central component of any administrator's reflective practice.

Epilogue

We hope that you have been convinced of Performance-Based Supervision and Evaluation's ability to integrate the most powerful aspects of educators' professional responsibilities and to make explicit both the processes and outcomes of learning, teaching, and leading. We have seen PBSE in action and have shared the journeys of teachers and administrators as they implemented the model. In our collective experience, PBSE's capacity to strategically and effectively encourage the growth of students, teachers, and administrators goes well beyond any other model we have seen or used.

And so we approach the final pages of this book not as a conclusion of the conversation, but as the beginning of many new and rich dialogues about teaching and learning. From that perspective, a discussion of conditions and initiatives that will best support teachers and administrators considering a performance-based approach to their practice is in order. What will it take to make PBSE work?

First, each district and school has unique strengths and challenges. In the real world, it is difficult to find perfect conditions for the adoption of any model of supervision and evaluation. PBSE is designed for the real world in that it builds both teachers' and administrators' capacity to improve student learning one classroom at a time, one school at a time. With that in mind, we believe that PBSE implementation is most likely to succeed when the following circumstances apply:

• *There is constancy of purpose.* The shift to working in a different way is demanding and complex, and so a dedicated focus on performance-based thinking and action is needed.

• *School and district leaders are committed to the model.* Without a mutual commitment to adopting PBSE, it is difficult to sustain the effort through a full process of change.

• *Teachers are involved in the decision to look at professional responsibilities from a more performance-based perspective.* As with any initiative, the more teachers participate in the change process, the more ownership and autonomy they will experience in their evolving practice.

• *There is ongoing support for the educators participating in PBSE.* This includes both the collegial support that derives from true collaboration and more tangible resources, such as materials, time, and professional development experiences.

• *The culture of the school and district embraces innovative practice.* PBSE educators need to work in an environment where they are free to try reasoned, strategic, and original approaches without fear of sanction.

• *The necessary time is provided and honored.* PBSE cannot take root overnight. Each school and district must allow that full implementation of this model will take a reasonable amount of time; the duration of the change process will vary from context to context.

• *Educators are willing to continue their professional growth.* Educators' ability to respond appropriately to student learning needs depends on their ability to use data effectively. Without skills in data collection, data analysis, and data interpretation, teachers cannot design relevant instructional interventions.

• *Educators are willing to collaborate.* Teachers and administrators must be open to making professional work explicit through collaborative dialogues around teaching, learning, and student work.

• *Educators see themselves and one another as resources.* Expertise and experiences—individual and collective—are vital tools within every school community. Educators must work together in new ways to help each other develop new skills.

There has never been a more important time to advocate for internal coherence within our work as educators or to commit ourselves to building our instructional capacity. Without a common vision and the knowledge and skills to affect student learning, there will be no improvement in student performance (Elmore, 2002). Experience has shown us that as a school or district increases its use of supervision for learning, these practices have an increasingly positive influence on student learning. These results, in turn, engender an even stronger desire to refine instructional practices further and fuel a deep sense of professional satisfaction. Performance-Based Supervision and Evaluation offers just such a pathway to success. We look forward to sharing more of these journeys with our fellow educators.

APPENDIX A

The Criteria of Excellence

Figure A.1
Criteria of Excellence for the Teacher Preparation Phase

Indicator	Criteria
TP-1 _____	*The teacher has identified* • Student performance data that represent "essential learning" and are standards-based.
TP-2 _____	• Student performance data that result from holistic assessment of a learning task requiring students to apply multiple skills and various knowledge.
TP-3 _____	*The teacher has organized* • Student performance data so that they may be viewed and interpreted in more than one way.
TP-4 _____	• Student performance data to reveal student performance strengths and weaknesses.
TP-5 _____	*The teacher has completed an analysis of data, producing* • Some conclusions about student performance strengths and weaknesses.
TP-6 _____	• Some artifacts of student work exemplifying student performance strengths and weaknesses.
TP-7 _____	• Some ideas about how to modify teaching to bring about improved student learning in the areas targeted in the data analysis.

Evaluation Scale: C = Competent; E = Emergent; JB = Just Beginning

Figure A.2
Criteria of Excellence for the Initial Collaboration Phase

Indicator	Criteria
	The teacher and supervisor have had conversation(s) producing
IC-1 _____	• A review of the teacher's initial data analysis and conclusions or ideas for improvement.
IC-2 _____	• Some expansion and extension of the teacher's initial data analysis.
IC-3 _____	• Some brainstorming of the elements of a professional development plan that is responsive to the data analysis.
IC-4 _____	• Some brainstorming of the elements of a professional development plan designed to support the teacher's efforts to improve (ideas for "getting smarter" and increasing capacity).
	The teacher and supervisor have agreed on
IC-5 _____	• A formal and detailed teacher improvement objective with a chronology of processes and outcomes stated in student-performance terms. This objective is developed by the teacher.
IC-6 _____	• A formal and detailed professional development plan crafted by the teacher.
IC-7 _____	• A general identification and description of the supervisory activities (observations, conferences, reviews of student work, etc.) to take place during the Initial Monitoring Phase.

Evaluation Scale: C = Competent; E = Emergent; JB = Just Beginning

Figure A.3
Criteria of Excellence for the Initial Monitoring Phase

Indicator	Criteria
IM-1 _____	*The teacher has* • Implemented the formal teacher improvement objective per Indicator IC-5.
IM-2 _____	• Implemented the formal professional development plan developed per Indicator IC-6.
IM-3 _____	• Communicated responsibly and appropriately with the supervisor on teacher improvement and professional development efforts, providing artifacts of task completion as required.
IM-4 _____	*The supervisor has* • Monitored, facilitated, and supported the teacher's efforts as identified and described under Indicator IC-7.

Evaluation Scale: C = Competent; E = Emergent; JB = Just Beginning

Figure A.4
Criteria of Excellence for the Mid-Cycle Review Phase

Indicator	Criteria
	The teacher has
MCR-1 ____	• Developed and submitted to the supervisor a progress report that includes artifacts documenting progress to date on the teacher improvement objective (reference Indicator IC-5).
MCR-2 ____	• Developed and submitted to the supervisor a progress report that includes artifacts documenting progress to date on the professional development plan (reference Indicator IC-6).
MCR-3 ____	• Gathered and submitted a sample of student work that provides performance-based evidence of student learning.
	The supervisor has
MCR-4 ____	• Organized information and data related to the teacher's work during the Initial Monitoring Phase, including observational notes already shared, and prepared it for reflection with the teacher.

Evaluation Scale: C = Competent; E = Emergent; JB = Just Beginning
Note: In this phase, the evaluation scale refers to the teacher's ability to demonstrate depth and breadth of comprehensiveness and professional reflection in responding to the above activities.

(continued)

Figure A.4   (*continued*)

Indicator	Criteria
MCR-5 _____	*The teacher and supervisor have* • Engaged in the mid-cycle conference and have together reviewed 1. The teacher's progress report on the teacher improvement objective. 2. The teacher's progress report on the professional development plan. 3. The teacher's submitted sample of student work, which provides data-based evidence of student learning. 4. The supervisor's prepared review of information and data related to the teacher's work to date.
MCR-6 _____	• Discussed appropriate revisions to the teacher improvement objective and the professional development action plan and have reached agreement on these changes.
MCR-7 _____	*The teacher has* • Revised the teacher improvement objective and professional development plan as agreed and submitted the updated documents to the supervisor.

Evaluation Scale: C = Competent; E = Emergent; JB = Just Beginning
Note: In this phase, the evaluation scale refers to the teacher's ability to demonstrate depth and breadth of comprehensiveness and professional reflection in responding to the above activities.

Indicator	Criteria
	Figure A.5 Criteria of Excellence for the Secondary Monitoring Phase
SM-1 _____	*The teacher has* • Implemented the teacher improvement objective, as potentially revised per the Mid-Cycle Conference.
SM-2 _____	• Implemented the professional development plan, as potentially revised per the Mid-Cycle Conference.
SM-3 _____	• Communicated responsibly and appropriately with supervisors on teacher improvement and professional development efforts, providing artifacts of task completion as required.
SM-4 _____	*The supervisor has* • Monitored, facilitated, and supported the teacher's efforts as identified and described under Indicator IC-7.
Evaluation Scale: C = Competent; E = Emergent; JB = Just Beginning	

Figure A.6
Criteria of Excellence for the Summative Review Phase

Indicator	Criteria

SR-1 _____	*The teacher has*
	
	• Developed and submitted to the supervisor a final report of progress that includes artifacts documenting work on the improvement objective and the professional development plan. The final report includes a written reflection with the following sections:
	
	1. Report of Professional Growth and Improvement
	    a. A statement of the improvement objective.
	    b. A narrative summary of accomplishments relative to the improvement objective.
	    c. An organized presentation of artifacts, including representative student work, which provide evidence of reported accomplishments.
	
	2. Reflection on Professional Growth and Development
	    a. A summary of professional growth and development to date relative to the current teacher improvement objective.
	    b. A self-analysis of work to be continued relative to the current teacher improvement objective.
	    c. A perspective on additional areas that might be included in future teacher improvement and professional development efforts.

SR-2 _____	*The teacher and supervisor have* • Engaged in the summative review conference, which consists of the following activities: 1. The teacher's oral review of and reflection on the final report of progress, the improvement objective, and the professional development plan.

Indicator	Criteria
	Figure A.6 *(continued)*
	2. The teacher's oral review of the self-evaluation portion of the final report of progress.

	3. The supervisor's review of
	   a. The teacher's reports of accomplishments with regard to the improvement objective and professional development plan.
	   b. The supervisor's prepared review of information and data related to the teacher's performance in general and in relation to professional growth.

	4. Consensus on the contents of the final evaluation summary report, including
	   a. A narrative summary of performance highlights
	   b. Commendations
	   c. Recommendations

SR-3 ____	*The supervisor has* • Written the final evaluation summary report according to agreement on Indicators SR-1 and SR-2.
SR-4 ____	*The teacher and supervisor have* • Met for the purpose of reading and signing off on the final evaluation summary report.

Evaluation Scale: C = Competent; E = Emergent; JB = Just Beginning

Note: In this phase, the evaluation scale refers to the teacher's ability to demonstrate depth and breadth of comprehensiveness and professional reflection in responding to the above activities.

APPENDIX B

Sample Artifacts

This appendix provides examples of the array of artifacts that mathematics teacher Eileen Blanchard would have developed during her first year of implementing the Performance-Based Supervision and Evaluation process. These documents serve as a record of Eileen's work and provide a cumulative portrait of teacher development over time.

Please bear in mind that the work represented here is that of a teacher who is developing her understanding of this process. We also understand that these materials do not represent a comprehensive review of key mathematics resources, nor do they portray the work of a teacher who is highly skilled in the development of standards-based mathematics materials.

End-of-Cycle Reflection

Eileen Blanchard   May 29

This has been a very challenging year for me. As a veteran teacher, I had fine-tuned my 7th grade math units and lessons according to the most recent district curriculum revision, which took place several years ago, and felt that the instruction in my classes reflected my experience and mathematics knowledge.

Our district's adoption of Performance-Based Supervision and Evaluation (PBSE) meant that we had to look differently at our teaching and at our students' learning. At first, I wasn't sure what we were supposed to do. I knew that it related to student performance data, but looking at test and quiz scores the way I always had wasn't enough to determine what my students really needed in order to advance their math understanding. My principal, Gary Mulholland, advised me to begin by searching online for resources linked to math standards. I did, but still felt unsure about how to proceed and avoided meeting with Gary for a few weeks.

After the holiday break, I decided it was time to figure out how the PBSE model could become a learning experience for my students and me. Some of my colleagues were already excited about it, and Gary was willing to be patient with my progress. I decided to revise my professional improvement objective to allow time for a more thorough investigation, and I was grateful that the district's math department chairperson, Charlie Ramirez (someone I had known only from a distance), was willing to work with me to support my efforts. I enjoyed working with Charlie, and his support and guidance have been invaluable.

Despite my rough start, I feel that I have grown significantly in my ability to teach in a way that is more connected to math standards and to help my students learn more authentic knowledge and skills. I still have a way to go, but I'm looking forward to next year, when I can build upon what I learned this year.

The documents that follow show different aspects of my professional growth throughout this last academic year. My final report of progress is presented first and is followed by other artifacts of my work this year, which are presented chronologically.

Final Report of Progress

Staff Member: Eileen Blanchard   School Year: 2005–2006
Primary Instructional Assignment: 7th Grade Mathematics
Secondary Instructional Assignment: None
Primary Supervisor: Gary Mulholland, Principal

SECTION I: REPORT OF PROFESSIONAL GROWTH AND IMPROVEMENT

A. Statement of the Improvement Objective for Your Current Professional Development Plan

I identified a need for my mathematics students to improve their abilities to solve complex problems involving fractions, decimals, and percents. My current professional development efforts are directed toward learning more about teaching and assessment methods in order to improve my teaching in these areas.

B. Review of the Most Current Professional Development Plan and Accomplishments

My complete professional development plan is attached: Yes: X   No:

Summary of Accomplishments
Briefly describe your most significant professional development accomplishments this year, with a reference to the artifacts of evidence that are attached. Summarize only those accomplishments for which you have supporting evidence and include a reference to specific artifacts. Please do not provide detail in this section; your artifacts will provide the detail. Present accomplishments in chronological order.

10/31. I completed a Web-based investigation of math standards related to fractions, decimals, and percents, increasing my understanding of how they determine what is "essential" for students to learn. (See "Summary of Web Search on Math Standards.")

2/12. I completed specific readings about math standards, which included the review of some literature describing the connections between standards and the state mastery test. (See "Memo to District Chairperson," dated 11/21.)

2/22. I completed an initial outline of a standards-based unit in math, which was reviewed and later approved by the principal and the district mathematics department chairperson. (See "Outline of Standards-Based Unit.")

4/15. I completed the writing of a standards-based unit in fractions, decimals, and percents, including a performance assessment and rubric, which was ready for use in the classroom and approved by the district mathematics department chairperson. (See "Professional Reflection on a Standards-Based Mathematics Unit on Fractions, Decimals, and Percents" and "A Standards-Based Mathematics Unit on Fractions, Decimals, and Percents.")

5/20. I completed a summary report of the assessment results after teaching the standards-based math unit I developed. The summary presented an analysis of performance data and my reflections on them. (See "Analysis of and Reflections on a Standards-Based Mathematics Unit" and "Examples of Student Work.")

5/20. I completed a log of my meetings and consultations with my district chairperson, complete with reflections. These meetings occurred from November through May. (See "Log of Meetings and Reflections on Collaboration Efforts.")

SECTION II. REFLECTION ON PROFESSIONAL GROWTH AND DEVELOPMENT

Summative Reflection

When I identified the area of fractions, decimals, and percents as one in which my students could improve, I did so without really thinking much about it. In my experience as a teacher, my fellow teachers and I have always had to find some area to work on for our professional development. I knew from the state mastery test results that "fractions, decimals, and percents" was an area that continues to give students difficulty, so I figured I would look into it. What I did not realize at the time was that it is not enough to simply teach students about fractions, decimals, and percents so they "get it" well enough to pass my test at the end of the unit. Honestly, that is the way I had always looked at it. After my professional development work this year, which helped me to really understand what standards are, I now realize that students must learn about fractions, decimals, and percents deeply enough to be able to apply them in complicated and real-life problems. To simply do isolated examples correctly on a test is not enough.

This new understanding and appreciation of what it means for students to learn essential knowledge and skills did not come quickly or easily. I really struggled this past fall with understanding the difference between the way I always taught math and the way I am beginning to see that it needs to be taught. I really appreciate the patience and guidance offered by my principal and district chairperson, Charlie Ramirez. With their help, and with the tremendous amount I learned from professional reading, I experienced one of the biggest shifts in my teaching career.

What really convinced me that this new approach to professional development was working was when I taught a unit on fractions, decimals, and percents this spring. I had developed the unit differently and had focused on what the standards say students need to know. After teaching it, I tested students by giving them a performance assessment I developed with Charlie Ramirez's help. It was a complex task that I never would have believed my students could handle. To my surprise and delight, most did very well, and I knew they had really learned.

My professional development experience this year has changed the way I view what needs to be taught and learned, and I look forward to continuing to learn how to incorporate my new perspective further into my teaching.

Ideas for Future Professional Development

Based on the progress I made this year (see previous section), I believe I need to continue my efforts. I would like to continue to pursue the broad goal of improving my teaching and student learning on concepts and skills related to fractions, decimals, and percents. This would mean refining the unit I developed this year, including making some changes in the assessment. I am not yet confident in rubric development. With another opportunity to apply these things in my classes, I know my teaching will continue to improve.

Submitted by ____*Eileen Blanchard*____

Date ____*May 21, 2006*____

Summary of Web Search on Math Standards

To: Gary Mulholland, Principal
From: Eileen Blanchard, Grade 7 Math
Re: Mathematics Standards Research
Date: October 31

At our meeting last month, you suggested that I research information on mathematics standards and how they relate to what my 7th grade math students are learning. Over the past two weeks, I've spent several hours looking for information on the Internet, and I am amazed at how much is out there!

I started at the Connecticut State Department of Education Web site: http://www.state.ct.us/sde/dtl/curriculum/currkey3.htm. The standards for mathematics are clearly outlined there. The 7th grade curriculum, which was developed by our math curriculum team several years ago, is arranged by topics that do not coordinate exactly with the way the standards are organized. If we're supposed to teach according to the standards, I'll have to look more closely at the units I've been using with my 7th graders. Maybe there are some aspects of the standards that we haven't covered in the past.

But even more interesting were the resources available through the National Council for Teachers of Mathematics. I found full information about the NCTM standards at http://standards.nctm.org, but this Web site also offers links to additional resources that can be applied directly in the classroom. One of my favorites was "NCTM Illuminations" (http://illuminations.nctm.org), a site that "illuminates" NCTM's vision for mathematics instruction by offering lesson plans and units categorized according to math standards and grade levels. For someone like me, who is new to the process of planning lessons within a standards framework, these were really helpful. I was especially interested in lessons related to decimals, fractions, and percents at the 7th grade level, as this was the curriculum area I think will become my area of focus.

While I was surfing around on the Internet, I also found an article called "Critical Issue: Implementing Curriculum, Instruction, and Assessment Standards in Mathematics" (http://www.ncrel.org/sdrs/areas/issues/contentt/cntareas/math/ma600.htm). The article gives an overview of how teachers have worked to develop meaningful standards-related learning experiences for math students. There is a real focus on problem solving and helping kids to use the math they are learning in class. That's not something we've had a lot of time for in my class, but I think it would be very important. The sample excerpts sharing teachers' experiences really seem to focus on understanding concepts, active learning, and real life applications. That really does seem to make sense.

Finally, I wandered onto a Web site that relates knowledge of mathematics to knowledge of technology. It offers information about the National Educational Technology Standards Project, otherwise know as "The NETS Project." This is sponsored by the International Society for Technology in Education (ISTE) and seems to focus on integrating curriculum with technology. With all we're hearing about technology these days, it's probably a good idea to think about what my 7th graders are learning from this perspective as well. The link to mathematics standards is available at http://cnets.iste.org/currstands/cstands-m.html.

Needless to say, this exercise has been an eye-opener. I knew of the NCTM standards, but because we had the curriculum developed several years ago, I just assumed that what I was teaching was fine. I'm wondering now if our students have enough hands-on experiences with problem-solving, and to what extent I should revise my 7th grade units. Gary, I'm going to keep on looking at these Internet resources, and at the materials you lent me from your office. I'm looking forward to meeting with you in two weeks to talk about where to go from there.

Eileen

Revised Professional Development Plan

Eileen Blanchard   January 28

Update to Gary. I have revised my professional development plan based on our recent discussion.

Eileen Blanchard's Professional Development Plan—Revised January 27

Plan for the Students	Time Line	Plan for the Teacher
	by October 3	• Initial meeting with supervisor to discuss PBSE.
	by October 15	• Begin broad, Web-based investigation of math standards; in particular, investigate state standards related to fractions, decimals, and percents. • Begin to gather 6th grade math scores on the state assessment.
	by October 31	• Meet with supervisor to discuss mathematics standards, state assessment scores, and hypotheses regarding potential focus for the professional development plan. • Investigate other local and statewide content experts and PD resources, activities, and readings related to math standards.
	by November 15	• Begin PD readings related to mathematics standards. • Meet with the district math department chairperson about learning how to develop standards-based math units and assessments.
	by November 30	• Determine specific standards-based knowledge and skills related to fractions, decimals, and percents (as seen through state assessment data and resources) and begin to analyze these data. • Draft a professional development plan.

(continued)

Eileen Blanchard's Professional Development Plan—Revised January 27   (continued)

Plan for the Students	Time Line	Plan for the Teacher
	by January 20	• Meet with supervisor and the district math department chairperson to revise the professional development focus.
	by February 28	• Continue to meet weekly with the district math department chairperson regarding standards-based math assessment. • Develop an outline of a standards-based mathematics unit. • Revise the professional development plan.
• Begin teaching the standards-based unit on fractions, decimals, and percents.	by March 15	• Meet with the district math department chairperson to review drafts of the unit assessment and rubric.
• Implement a standards-based assessment on fractions, decimals, and percents. Use a standards-based rubric to score the assessment.	by April 15	• Meet with district math department chairperson to analyze the results of the unit performance assessment. • Meet with supervisor to review this analysis and share student work. • Schedule and conduct formal observations by supervisor and the district math department chairperson.
• Implement a second standards-based math unit and assessment. • Use a standards-based rubric to score the assessment.	by May 15	• Develop a second standards-based math unit, assessment, and rubric. • Analyze assessment results with the district math department chairperson.
	by May 30	• Meet with supervisor and the district math department chairperson for the summative review meeting. Present student work and artifacts from the professional development plan work.

Memo to the District Chairperson

To: Charlie Ramirez
From: Eileen Blanchard, Grade 7 Math
Re: Summary of Professional Development Resources
Date: February 12

Thanks again for the support you've given me as I work to find out more about math standards and how to use them to plan for instruction in my classes. Since we last spoke, I have investigated a number of journal articles and other resources related to the focus of my improvement objective: helping my students to understand and be able to use fractions, decimals, and percents. Most of the articles I mention in the following report are broad and related to standards-based curriculum or state assessments. As you know, I wanted to begin there because I did not have a strong understanding of what was happening with math standards and how they would affect my teaching.

As I look back over what I've read, I can see some themes across these resources. First, all the articles talk about providing quality math experiences for *all* students. I can see that this will mean more active engagement in math lessons and assessments, as well as more thinking about whether or not our district math curriculum is comprehensive, cohesive, and challenging. Other themes that come through involve establishing a classroom culture to support math learning, multiple ways to solve math problems, and an emphasis on making sense of applied math. I also have to think about my part in this: how can *I* contribute to a comprehensive, cohesive, and challenging curriculum? It's exciting to read about what is happening all over the world with math instruction.

I guess my overall major learning is that there is a need for balance in the "math wars." There are good reasons why the traditional, direct approach to math instruction, which is what I'm used to, works— particularly for teaching computation. But there is also much to be said for thinking about math ideas more deeply (with more integration) and more comprehensively (though application to real-life situations). I see that I should revise some of my lessons and some of my assessments to better balance the two. All of this is a bit overwhelming, but I can see that it is both necessary and exciting. Thank you for continuing to help me make progress with this initiative.

Eileen

Summary of Professional Development Readings

Bay, J. M., Reys, B., & Reys, R. E. (1999). The top 10 elements that must be in place to implement standards-based mathematics curricula. *Phi Delta Kappan, 80*(7), 503–506. As a result of their work with a number of middle school mathematics teachers in the Missouri Middle School Mathematics Project, the authors acknowledge that the change toward a more standards-based curriculum is difficult. They cite 10 elements of implementation that are critical to the success of a standards-based curriculum: (1) administrative support; (2) opportunities for teachers to study the standards; (3) opportunities for teachers to try out standards-based materials; (4) daily planning time for teachers; (5) the opportunity for teachers to interact with standards-based math experts; (6) time for teachers to collaborate with colleagues; (7) the use of new, standards-based forms of assessment; (8) proactive communication with parents; (9) support for students to adjust the way they view math; and (10) planning time for the transition.

Ferrini-Mundy, J. (2001). Introduction: Perspectives on principles and standards for school mathematics. *School Science and Mathematics, 101*(6), 277–279. This article was the introduction for a special issue of the journal *School Science and Mathematics* and focused on the NCTM *Principles and Standards for School Mathematics*. The author served as the chair of the entire writing group, which developed this revision of the original standards document. This article would be a good place to begin an investigation of the standards because it provides an overview of the development of NCTM standards and the impact that they have had on other content areas. The changes made in the second edition of the standards are highlighted; most significantly, the document now includes the principles underlying the standards; that is, the perspectives that guided the development of the revised standards. This was considered important because the wide debate about the original standards had evoked many interpretations about what the underlying principles might have been.

Harris, K., Marcus, R., & McLaren, K. (2001). Curriculum materials supporting problem-based teaching. *School Science and Mathematics, 101*(6), 310–318. This article was an eye-opener! It focused on problem solving within a standards-based curriculum and how it would differ from traditional problem solving. Standards-based problem solving involves rich and complex problems that give rise to deep thinking about mathematical concepts. The problems are interesting to students, offer teachers a chance to see how much prior knowledge the students have, encourage students to collaborate in finding solutions (sometimes more than one), and support students as they discover the important math concepts embedded in the problem. The article offers three examples of rich problems and demonstrates how the problem can be used to introduce the topic, explore the topic in greater depth, help students share their reasoning and insights, and extend the concept. Having materials like these is important, but the skillfulness of the teacher is also critical to effective standards-based problem solving. When this approach is used, however, students demonstrate deeper conceptual understanding, use a broader variety of strategies for problem solving and calculation, and outperform students in a more traditional program.

Herrera, T. A., & Owens, D. T. (2001). The new math? Two reform movements in mathematics education. *Theory into Practice, 40*(2), **84–92.** The authors compare the movement known as "the new math" and standards-based math curriculum. Both seek to extend math content and both, although initially received with enthusiasm, later met criticism and opposition. However, the new math focuses on deductive reasoning and rigorous proof and abstraction, while standards-based math strongly emphasizes constructivism and application to real-life contexts.

Jacob, B. (2001). Implementing standards: The California mathematics textbook debacle. *Phi Delta Kappan, 83*(3), **264–272.** This article appeared in an issue of *Phi Delta Kappan* and focused on the "math wars": the debate over a standards-based approach to mathematics vs. a more traditional approach. The focus of the article is a chronological account of mathematics textbook adoptions in California from 1997–2001, and the very political influences that affected these decisions. Development of a mathematics framework, high-stakes testing, and textbook adoption lists moved from a more collaborative process involving teacher input to a closed-door process influenced by elected officials. As a result, the author asserts, the state framework and approved curriculum materials offer little opportunity for California's children to understand mathematical concepts deeply.

Loveless, T., & Coughlan, J. (2004). The arithmetic gap. *Educational Leadership, 61*(5), **55–59.** The authors examine longitudinal performance in mathematics as measured by the National Assessment of Educational Progress (NAEP), and conclude that computation skills, especially those of older students, have diminished over time. The authors make the case that the ability to add, subtract, multiply, and divide is important for whole numbers, fractions, and decimals. They base this on the following assertions:
• Accurate computation is essential to the advancement of math and science. Students who do not have basic math skills cannot do more advanced math or science.

• More and more, basic computation skills are a predictor of adult earning. In the workplace, basic math skills are essential.
• Computation skills support equity. Declining computation skills raise concerns about racial inequity, further widening the achievement gap.

These authors blame the decline in basic computation skills on three factors: (1) poor preparation for math teachers, especially at the elementary and middle school level; (2) increasing use of calculators; and (3) the standards-based math reform movement of the 1990s. They advocate a return to basic proficiency in computation for all students.

Oster, E., Graudgenett, N., McGlamery, S., & Topp, N. (1999). How to avoid common problems and misunderstandings of the NCTM standards. *Education* **(Chula Vista, CA),** *120*(2), **397–400.** Although the authors see the NCTM standards as well-crafted and well-intended, they advocate a more balanced approach to math literacy and offer a "top 10" list of mistakes *not* to make when implementing a standards-based approach to teaching math: (1) teach only the math in the mathematics curriculum; (2) let the textbook drive instruction; (3) use manipulatives, but don't connect them to math. (4) basic skills first, then higher order thinking; (5) ignore the outcomes developed by your district; (6) instruction and assessment are separate; (7) technology and instruction are separate; (8) all teachers should teach in the same way; (9) all content should be taught in the same order; (10) follow the expert's advice (or the authors') too closely. The authors commend the role of the teacher in interpreting the district curriculum within the context of NCTM standards.

Reys, R. (2001). Curricular controversy in the math wars: A battle without winners. *Phi Delta Kappan, 83*(3), **255–258.** The author comments that the math wars take up a great deal of energy and emotion that would be better spent developing stronger mathematics programs to meet students' needs. The article cites the slow pace of any kind of change in mathematics instruction, driven by (1) the tendency to hold on to a more traditional approach; (2) the significant influence of textbook publishers, who are reluctant to develop radically different products; and (3) the variability of mathematics teaching and learning across the country. Also cited is the need for continuing research into standards-based math curricula and programs.

Reys, R., Reys, B., & Lapan, R. (2003). Assessing the impact of standards-based middle grades mathematics curriculum materials on student achievement. *Journal for Research in Mathematics Education, 34*(1), **74–95.** This article reports the findings of a research study conducted through a grant from the National Science Foundation. The focus of the two-year study was to follow and compare the math performance of two groups of 8th grade students in Missouri: one group used standards-based curriculum materials and the other group used more traditional materials. Students using standards-based materials scored higher on the math portion of the Missouri Assessment Program than those who did not used a standards-based curriculum. In the areas of data analysis and algebra, these differences were statistically significant.

Schmidt, W. H. (2004, February). A vision for mathematics. *Educational Leadership, 61***(5), 6–11.** The author argues for a common, coherent, and challenging mathematics curriculum as the key element in strengthening math instruction for students in the United States. First, there should be a common math curriculum, as is the case in high-performing countries, according to the Trends in International Mathematics and Science Study (TIMSS). *All* children should have the same opportunities to learn at high levels. Second, the curriculum should identify a coherent progression of learning that reflects the cumulative nature of mathematics. Finally, the mathematics curriculum should be challenging, including the introduction of topics in algebra and geometry at the middle school level. The article presents two figures that depict the sequence of math topics in high-performing countries vs. the less coherent sequence seen in the math curriculum from three sample states. The importance of teacher preparation for delivering a common, coherent, and challenging math curriculum is also discussed.

Schoen, H., Fey, J. T., & Hirsch, C. R. (1999). Issues and options in the math wars. *Phi Delta Kappan, 80***(6), 444–453.** This article offers an overview of issues related to the "math wars," including a chronological review of the reform movement and later opposition. The article also discusses the Core-Plus Mathematics Project (CPMP), one of several standards-based efforts funded by the National Science Foundation, and the positive effect the CPMP had on student learning. Although these findings were encouraging, more research is needed on reform curricula.

Silver, E. A. (2000). Improving mathematics teaching and learning: How can principles and standards help? *Mathematics Teaching in the Middle School, 6***(1), 20–23.** The author of this article was the leader of the 6–8 Standards Writing group for the development of the *Principles and Standards for School Mathematics* (2000). He argues that to improve student understanding of mathematical concepts, middle schoolers need to "engage on a regular basis with well-designed, carefully sequenced, challenging problems and experiences that develop mathematical understanding and proficiency within topic areas and with appropriate connections across topics" (p. 21). Discrete units on different math topics are ultimately inferior to a more integrated approach, which will develop understanding of many topics over time. Using a Circle-in-the-Square problem, the article shows how one problem can be used to develop understanding of rational numbers, ratios and proportions, algebra, and geometry. The author also asserts that students need to be able to think flexibly and accurately about fractions, decimals, and percents (my area of interest).

Stigler, J. W., & Hiebert, J. (2004, February). Improving mathematics teaching. *Educational Leadership, 61*(5), 12–17. This was a very interesting article. The authors discussed two TIMSS video studies in which 8th grade mathematics classrooms in several countries were videotaped to discover how math was taught in different cultures. The U.S. participated in both studies. The 1995 video study produced the following findings: (1) Educators have a lack of common language to use when discussing professional knowledge. This makes it hard to share ideas or generate new ones. (2) What was seen in the videotapes was generally different from what the established policy was in each country. Although reform ideas were known to classroom teachers, their implementation of new strategies remained very uneven. (3) Teaching in each country was a cultural phenomenon. Despite random selection of classrooms, there was a strong homogeneity of teaching methods observed in each country, and these varied from country to country.

With this information as a foundation, the researchers conducted another study in 1999, this time with more and different countries (although the United States participated in both research projects). The findings from the second study were even more striking: (1) There are many forms of effective teaching. Improving student achievement is not reliant on finding the one "right" model; many models can serve as sources of effective instruction. (2) What affects student learning is not so much the organization of the lesson or the materials used, but the way in which instruction is implemented. The article includes a figure depicting that when the researchers looked at problem solving in U.S. classrooms, there was a distinct reliance on procedures rather than deep thinking and making connections to develop a solution. This is in stark contrast to other countries.

As a result of these studies, the authors suggest three ideas to improve classroom teaching in math in the United States: (1) Focus on improving teaching, rather than teachers. (2) Be aware of cultural routines in order to make changes in teaching. (3) Continue to build a knowledge base of "theories, empirical research, and alternative images of what implementation looks like" (p. 16).

Trafton, P. R., Reys, B., & Wasman, D. (2001). Standards-based mathematics materials: A phrase in search of definition. *Phi Delta Kappan, 83*(3), 259–264. The authors say that in order to implement a math-standards approach to teaching, using appropriate and standards-based materials will be critical. They identify six characteristics of materials that would be truly standards-based:

1. *Comprehensiveness.* The resources used daily in math classes should equip students with a broad understanding of important math ideas, which effectively prepare students to enter the workforce and to pursue higher levels of math instruction, should they wish to do so.
2. *Coherence.* Math materials should represent important core ideas in such a way that they are understood deeply on their own, and also seen as a part of an integrative whole. The relationships and connections among the ideas are as important as the ideas themselves.
3. *Depth.* Instead of covering many math topics in a shallow way, standards-based materials should encourage deep understanding of math concepts, particularly over time as the students' mathematic knowledge matures.
4. *Sense-making.* Traditional math materials encouraged rote memorization of processes with little focus on how and why these processes work. A standards-based approach requires resources that help students to make sense out of what they are learning and connect their knowledge and skills to real life.
5. *Engagement.* Standards-based resources should engage students intellectually and physically. Intellectual engagement is encouraged by tasks that are complex enough to be hard but fun, and which result in students thinking divergently and creatively. These tasks should also be both interesting and achievable by students who are asked to do them. Manipulatives help students to be physically engaged in mathematics learning and to see a concrete representation of ideas and processes.
6. *Motivation for learning.* The new approach to math embeds many more applications of mathematics into lessons and units. This allows students to understand why the knowledge and skills are useful and why they are learning them.

To use standards-based math materials effectively, teachers will need appropriate and on-going professional development. The authors agree that this must take place over an extended period of time before a teacher may feel comfortable enough to use a fully standards-based approach to teaching mathematics.

Weiss, I., & Pasley, J. (2004, February). What is high-quality instruction? *Educational Leadership, 61*(5), **24–28.** This article emerged from an 18-month research study called *Inside the Classroom,* conducted by the authors and additional colleagues in 2003. The study examined instruction in math and science and generally found a lack of rigor in most of the 364 lessons observed. As a result of the study, the authors developed the following profile of a high-quality classroom:

- There is a high level of student engagement with the content, involving students and building on their previous knowledge.
- There is a classroom culture conducive to learning, meaning that students are challenged to think deeply and are encouraged to contribute their ideas freely.
- All students have access to high-quality instruction, and safeguards are present to provide this to those who would otherwise be left out.
- Teachers use effective questioning skills to encourage students to think deeply about content ideas.
- Teachers help students "make sense" out of what they are learning by providing clear explanations and opportunities to make connections.

The article recommends that teachers be aware of the external influences on classroom content, and select instructional strategies carefully. In addition, to be effective in the classroom, teachers need (1) supports, such as clear, important, and developmentally appropriate learning goals; (2) the opportunity to analyze their lessons within the framework of high-quality instruction; (3) appropriate instructional materials; and (4) relevant professional development.

Overview of a Standards-Based Mathematics Unit

Eileen Blanchard   February 22

Update to Gary. Thank you for your patience as I get back on track with my professional objective this year. I have begun meeting with Charlie Ramirez to make both my teaching and my students' learning more connected to math standards. We have come up with an idea for a standards-based math unit, which I hope to implement later this year.

As you know, I have been concerned about my students' performance on the state mastery test for some time, especially in the area of fractions, decimals, and percents. Charlie and I have brainstormed ideas for a unit on this topic. So far, this unit would include the following:

• Hands-on learning, to reflect the growing trend toward a more constructivist approach to student learning.
• Teaching and learning that appeal to multiple learning modalities (visual, auditory, and kinesthetic modes).
• The opportunity to apply previous learning. The plan is to teach this unit after my individual, existing units on fractions, decimals, and percents, and it would connect these three areas and ask students to apply math skills to real-life situations.

While researching math standards, especially those for fractions, decimals, and percents, I saw that many math teachers use something called a "10 × 10 grid" or "hundredths grid." It's a square that divided 10 × 10 into 100 blocks and is used as a tool to help students visualize parts of a whole and how $\frac{1}{4}$ of the entire matrix is also equal to .25 or 25 percent. Charlie and I plan to use a 10 × 10 grid as the basis for our new unit to teach equivalent fractions and the links among fractions, decimals, and percents. We're also going to measure the students' ability to apply this knowledge by developing an end-of-unit performance assessment that will pull everything together.

I'm a little nervous about teaching in this different way, but also kind of excited to finally be doing something about the standards. I'm also grateful to have Charlie's support and help in actually developing this new unit and planning for its implementation. We'll be sure to give you a copy of the unit when it's finished.

Eileen

Professional Reflection on a Standards-Based Mathematics Unit on Fractions, Decimals, and Percents

Eileen Blanchard   April 15

Together with Charlie Ramirez, the district's mathematics department chairperson, I have been working for several weeks to construct a math unit that pulls together the individual units I have already covered on fractions, decimals, and percents, and link them more explicitly to the relevant state standards for mathematics. This has not been easy for me, because it is a much different way to teach than what I have been used to. My earlier investigations this year have been around discovering the standards and exploring a constructivist way to teach math (making math as "hands-on" as possible for my students and leading them to "discover" the concepts and processes, rather than just telling them what to do). I can see that for many students, this approach results in more student engagement, but there are still a few children who just want to be told what they are supposed to do and are unsure how to learn independently. I guess we'll have to learn how to do that together.

When I was reading about standards-based mathematics units on fractions, decimals, and percents, I saw that a number of math teachers used a tool known as a "10 × 10 grid" or "hundredths grid" to help students visualize the relationships among fractions, decimals, and percents. That made a lot of sense to me, because it equalizes all three concepts, so I've used it as the foundation for this unit. In regard to the quality of the unit, I'm still not sure if it is too challenging for my 7th graders or perhaps not challenging enough for some of them. Fractions, decimals, and percents persist as an area of lower performance for my 7th graders on state tests. But at the same time, I think they *should* know how to do math at this level, and maybe even at a higher level. I just need the time and support to help my students learn at higher levels, and I am willing to put energy into doing just that. I appreciate the extra time and effort the district mathematics chairperson has dedicated to working with me on this project!

A Standards-Based Unit on Fractions, Decimals, and Percents for 7th Grade Mathematics

Eileen Blanchard

This unit of instruction was designed to follow three traditional instructional units focused individually on fractions, decimals, and percents, and to help students conceptualize the relationship among these three forms of mathematical expression.

Unit Objectives
1. Students will identify equivalent fractions, decimals, and percents.
2. Students will select the most appropriate methods for computing fractions, decimals, and percents.
3. Students will work flexibly with fractions, decimals, and percents.
4. Students will demonstrate the ability to apply fractions, decimals, and percents through a performance-based assessment.

Connection to State Mathematics Standards
This unit addresses state mathematics standards related to fractions, decimals, and percents, as seen in the Number Sense and Operations standards and content strands of the Connecticut Framework K–12 Curricular Goals and Standards.

Day One: The Relationship Among Fractions, Decimals, and Percents

Materials needed: Dry erase board and dry erase markers, grid practice sheets, crayons or marking pens

1. At the dry erase board, connect to previous knowledge by constructing a three-column "K-W-L" chart focused on fractions, decimals, and percents. Prompt the students to contribute to the "What I know" and "What I want to learn" columns.
2. Introduce the 10 × 10 Grid Practice Sheet (a prepared handout with 8 numbered 10 × 10 grids). Ask students to look carefully at the grids. What do they observe? What characteristics do all eight grids have in common?
3. Discuss the notion of a whole unit—the grid—as the sum of 10 × 10, or 100. The concept of 100 is the common basis for understanding equivalent fractions, decimals, and percents.
4. Using an overhead projector and a transparency of the Single Grid Sheet, divide the grid into four equal parts. Count how many squares are in one of the four parts. Model coloring in 25 squares as 25 percent, .25, or $\frac{1}{4}$ of the grid, asking students to do the same on Grid #1 on their Grid Practice Sheets.

5. Repeat the modeling, this time using 60 grids to represent 60 percent, .60, and $\frac{60}{100}$.
6. Ask what students observe from this process. What additional questions do they have?
7. *Guided Practice Activity:* In pairs, students will work together to complete the following table for the eight practice grids on a second Grid Practice Sheet, using the information provided to obtain the remaining information needed:

Grid	# Squares to Color	Fraction Equals $\frac{x}{100}$	Decimal Equivalent	Percent Equivalent
1	40			
2	65			
3		$\frac{14}{100}$		
4		$\frac{85}{100}$		
5			.27	
6			.53	
7				30%
8				74%

8. *Closure Discussion:* "What have we discovered about the relationship among fractions, decimals, and percents?"

Homework: Create your own table, similar to the one you used in the guided practice activity. It should show eight different amounts expressed as fractions, decimals, and percents. Using a new Practice Grid Sheet, color in a corresponding grid for each of the eight amounts

Day Two: Equivalent Fractions to Support Computation

1. *Paired Student Discussions:* Students share and compare the grids they created for homework. (10 minutes)
2. *Whole-Class Discussion:* "What do we recall about the relationships among fractions, decimals, and percents?" Collect student homework.
3. Using an overhead projector and a transparency of the 10 × 10 Single Grid Sheet, review equivalent fractions with students. Returning to yesterday's problem of $\frac{1}{4}$ = 25 percent = .25, how many squares on the practice grid sheet represent $\frac{1}{4}$ of the entire grid? How would we express that in hundredths?
4. Ask students what would happen if we needed to add fractions that had different denominators, for example $\frac{1}{10}$ and $\frac{3}{5}$? (*Note:* Use only

denominators that are divisible into 100.) Have students once again work in pairs to brainstorm methods for combining fractions with unlike denominators. Use the dry erase board to record their responses, working through both appropriate and problematic methods with the example of $\frac{1}{10}$ and $\frac{3}{5}$. When necessary, use a Practice Grid Sheet transparency and an overhead projector to color in squares that represent the equivalent of a fraction.

5. Model the addition of two more pairs of unlike fractions: $\frac{1}{20} + \frac{5}{50}$, and $\frac{7}{20} + \frac{3}{10}$. What happens when the two fractions added together are more than one? Model adding $\frac{8}{10} + \frac{4}{5}$.

6. *Guided Practice Activity:* Each pair of students will create two examples of adding together two fractions with unlike denominators, and demonstrate these on a practice grid, using different colors to represent each fraction.

7. *Closure Discussion:* "How does the practice grid sheet help us to see how fractions with different denominators can be added? What does it tell us about the relationship among fractions, decimals, and percents?"

Homework: Interview your mom, dad, or another adult family member. What are some examples of times when they have had to work with calculations that included a mixture of fractions, decimals, and percents?

Day Three: Initial Application of Fractions/Decimals/Percents to Real Life

1. Conduct a whole-class discussion to debrief the homework interviews. List examples of applied mixed measures on the board.

2. On the dry erase board, write the following challenge problem for students to work on independently. Ask them calculate the answer, and then write a narrative reflection of how they arrived at that answer.

    A 7th grade class has 100 students and is conducting a food drive to benefit the local food bank. Collection of nonperishable food items will take place over a five-day period, and students have been asked to bring in just one food item per day. By the end of the week, 24 percent had brought in five canned items, a third of the class had brought four items, .13 of the class had contributed three items, a tenth had brought two items, and 15 percent had brought one item. How many nonperishable items will the class bring to the food bank?"

3. As a whole class, debrief the correct answer (326) by following how one student arrived at the total number of items, then discovering *other ways* in which students calculated the correct answer.

4. *Closure Activity:* Return to the opening activity of the unit: the K-W-L chart. Focus on the third column and list on the dry erase board what students have learned through this integrative unit.

Homework: Review in your math notebook the materials from the units on fractions, decimals, and percents, as well as the work done this week in preparation for a performance assessment tomorrow.

Day Four: Performance Assessment

Students will complete an in-class, individual performance assessment task.

Materials: Directions for the task and several copies per student of a single, enlarged 10 x 10 grid.

Task Prompt: The Fairview Middle School Parent–Teacher Organization (PTO) has decided to take on a school service project to beautify the grounds at the school—specifically a small area to the left of the driveway leading to the school parking lot. The area in which they would like to plant flowers is 10 feet by 10 feet. The PTO was able to obtain donations of flowers and bulbs from local nurseries and florists. Now, there will be a contest, open only to 7th graders, for the most creative design for a flower bed.

Here are the guidelines:
1. There must be a one-foot path between sections of different flowers.
2. There are 10 daylily bulbs. These bulbs will grow to be tall flowers, and they must be planted one foot apart.
3. Reserve .15 of the garden for daffodils. Daffodil bulbs grow into medium-height flowers.
4. Reserve 25 percent of the garden for wildflower seeds. These seeds grow into medium-height flowers.
5. The PTO would like to plant the shorter pansies and petunias on $\frac{1}{5}$ of the flower bed, to complement the other plants.

Use the following key for marking your squares to indicate where you will place the flowers: DL = Daylilies; DAF = Daffodils; WF = Wildflowers; PP = Pansies and Petunias

When you have finished your design, write an explanation of your work and how you determined the final design. Submit your design and explanation at the end of this class period. Good luck in the contest!

Analysis of and Reflections on a Standards-Based Mathematics Unit

Eileen Blanchard   May 20

The following represents my efforts to develop an analysis of the work that the students in my Period G class did on a performance-based assessment, which was the culmination of the standards-based, integrated unit I taught on fractions, decimals, and percents.

As a result of my collaboration with Charlie Ramirez to create a more performance-based assessment for fractions, decimals, and percents, I came to understand that I would need a rubric to assess my students' responses to the task on this unit's assessment. Earlier in the year, I had investigated the state department of education Web site and discovered not only the state math standards, but what are called the "trace maps" for mathematics. These are specific lists of mathematics knowledge and skills that students in our state should know and be able to use at different grade levels. I looked through these lists for grades 6 and 7 and selected four skills related to fractions, decimals, and percents in order to create a more standards-based rubric to score the performance assessment. With Charlie's help, I created the rubric in Figure A.

The 18 students in my Period G class completed the unit assessment last week, and I scored their papers using the rubric. An amazing number of things happened as a result. First, I did get a sense of their competence—as a group and individually—with these skills. I coded the papers so that I would not be influenced by students' names as I applied the rubric. Charlie recommended that I begin my data analysis with a simple table depicting the scores of each student. See Figure B.

Charlie and I decided to set a high standard for proficiency. Students had to earn a score of 4 or better in each of the four skills related to this performance assessment in order to be "proficient" overall for this assessment.

Many understandings and ideas have emerged from this process. First, and probably my biggest insight, is that the analysis helped me to understand my students' growth individually and as a group. I can tell that my students "get it" when it comes to equivalent fractions, decimals, and percents because their scores reflect fairly consistent accuracy with different forms of equivalents. But when they are asked to apply this knowledge in the context of related knowledge and skills, some fall short, and I know I need to address this. In Figure C, I've listed the names of the kids who will need additional support and attention, along with their scores on each element of the rubric.

It's clear that the six students I've identified know how to convert equivalent fractions, decimals, and percents, but applying this knowledge to a problem is still challenging for them. I will look to Charlie

Figure A: Rubric for Scoring the Performance-Based Assessment on Fractions, Decimals, and Percents

Skill 1: Represent fractions, mixed numbers, decimals, and percents in a variety of equivalent forms, using concrete, pictorial, and symbolic representations. (*Standard: Number Sense*)

5	4	3	2	1
The design and explanation demonstrate clear knowledge of equivalency for fractions, decimals, and percents	For the most part, the design and explanation demonstrate clear knowledge of equivalency for fractions, decimals, and percents	The design and explanation demonstrate general understanding of equivalent fractions, decimals, and percents	There is minimal evidence for equivalency of fractions, decimals, and percents	There is little or no evidence for equivalency of fractions, decimals, and percents

Skill 2: Work flexibly with fractions, decimals, and percents to solve problems. (*Standard: Number Sense*)

5	4	3	2	1
The design and explanation show that the student is consistently able to work flexibly with fractions, decimals, and percents to solve the problem accurately	The design and explanation show that the student is able to work flexibly with fractions, decimals, and percents to solve the problem accurately most of the time	The design and explanation show that the student is generally able to work flexibly with fractions, decimals, and percents to solve the problem accurately	The design and explanation show that the student is minimally able to work flexibly with fractions, decimals, and percents to solve the problem accurately	Evidence of the student's ability to work flexibly with fractions, decimals, and percents to solve the problem is limited

Skill 3: Develop fluency with all operations for whole numbers, decimals, and fractions and mixed numbers. (*Standard: Operations*)

5	4	3	2	1
The design and explanation provide clear evidence that the student is fluent in all operations involving fractions, decimals, and percents	For the most part, the design and explanation demonstrate fluency in all operations involving fractions, decimals, and percents	The design and explanation demonstrate general fluency in all operations involving fractions, decimals, and percents	The design and explanation demonstrate minimal fluency in all operations involving fractions, decimals, and percents	Evidence of fluency in all operations involving fractions, decimals, and percents is limited

Skill 4: Solve problems involving ratio, proportion, and percent. (*Standard: Ratios, Proportions, and Percents*)

5	4	3	2	1
The design and explanation very clearly demonstrate an ability to solve problems involving ratio, proportion, and percents	The design and explanation demonstrate an ability to solve problems involving ratio, proportion, and percents most of the time	The design and explanation demonstrate a general ability to solve problems involving ratio, proportion, and percents	The design and explanation demonstrate minimal ability to solve problems involving ratio, proportion, and percents	Evidence of the ability to solve problems involving ratio, proportion, and percents is limited

Figure B: Initial Analysis of Student Performance Data on the Performance-Based Assessment on Fractions, Decimals, and Percents

Student	Skill 1	Skill 2	Skill 3	Skill 4	Met Proficiency?
A	5	4	N/A	4	Yes
B	4	4	N/A	4	Yes
C	4	4	N/A	4	Yes
D	5	5	N/A	5	Yes
E	5	2	N/A	2	No
F	4	3	N/A	3	No
G	5	4	N/A	4	Yes
H	4	4	N/A	4	Yes
I	4	3	N/A	3	No
J	5	5	N/A	4	Yes
K	4	2	N/A	2	No
L	4	4	N/A	4	Yes
M	5	5	N/A	5	Yes
N	5	4	N/A	4	Yes
O	4	2	N/A	2	No
P	5	5	N/A	5	Yes
Q	4	4	N/A	4	Yes
R	4	2	N/A	2	No
AVG	**4.44**	**3.67**	—	**3.61**	—

Note: Skill 1: *Equivalent Forms of Fractions, Decimals, and Percents;* Skill 2: *Work Flexibly with Fractions, Decimals, and Percents to Solve Problems;* Skill 3: *Fluency with Operations for Fractions, Decimals, and Percents;* Skill 4: *Solve Problems with Ratios, Proportions, and Percents*

for help developing a plan to work more closely with these students on that skill.

Second, this analysis gave me some insight into the effectiveness of the performance-based assessment I developed for fractions, decimals, and percents. When I worked with Charlie to create this unit, the entire process was new to me, and I thought the unit looked great. But developing and using the rubric, based on the skills related to our state standards, showed me that I had left out an important piece in the assessment: when I asked students to create a layout for the flower bed, they simply needed to recognize and apply several fractions, decimals, and percents. There was no opportunity to use any operations to calculate numbers! Because of this omission, I scored that part of the rubric "N/A," but I'll need to go back and revise the assessment task to make it more challenging for future use. Now that I think more about the assessment

Figure C: Students Who Need Support with Fractions, Decimals, and Percents

Student	Skill 1	Skill 2	Skill 3	Skill 4	Met Proficiency?
Yvonne	5	2	N/A	2	No
Frank	4	3	N/A	3	No
Carmela	4	3	N/A	3	No
Rich	4	2	N/A	2	No
Barbara	4	2	N/A	2	No
Debra	4	2	N/A	2	No

Note: Skill 1: Equivalent Forms of Fractions, Decimals, and Percents; Skill 2: Work Flexibly with Fractions, Decimals, and Percents to Solve Problems; Skill 3: Fluency with Operations for Fractions, Decimals, and Percents; Skill 4: Solve Problems with Ratios, Proportions, and Percents

task, I also realize that there should also be more of an emphasis on higher-order thinking skills. I will talk with Charlie about how to include this in the assessment at our next meeting. I'm concerned that the assessment, and maybe even the unit itself, was not challenging enough.

Third, this process has given me the opportunity to think about the rubric developed to score student work on the performance assessment. While the rubric was useful, I see now that it could certainly be improved. When I applied it to student work, the scores for the second skill (working flexibly with fractions, decimals, and percents to solve problems) and the fourth skill (solving problems with ratios, proportions, and percents) tended to be the same. Maybe these overlap, or perhaps I can be clearer about how they are different? The other thing I would do to improve the rubric is related to the evaluation criteria. When I first created the rubric, I based the evaluation criteria on the state "trace maps," which describe specific skills that students should have at my grade level. But I keep thinking about those articles I read last fall. The literature recommends math activities and assessments that are interesting, complex, and coherent. I'd like to go back and revise my assessment task to be more like that, and I think the rubric should also include elements that look for coherence and higher-order thinking in student work. I should also be looking at how students make sense of their work, especially math applications to real life. On this assessment, I found that kind of information came through in my students' *explanations* of their work more than in the designs they created. If I scheduled more time for the assessment, maybe two days instead of one, I might even ask students to create two or three versions of their responses to see how they might approach the problem from different directions.

All in all, the process of using a standards-based assessment and looking at student work more deeply has been a real eye-opener for me. The analysis above is certainly different than what I used to do: grade papers and enter the scores into my grade book! It's more work, but well worth it, and I know I can be even more specific with my analysis as I continue to learn more about this process. I'm hoping that Charlie will continue to work with me on that.

At Charlie's recommendation, I've attached three examples of my students' work on the performance task to illustrate what I consider to be a strong response, a mostly correct response, and weaker response to the assessment task.

Examples of Student Work

Student D's Work: Proficient Response (Strong and Clear)

DL	DL	DL	DL	DL	DL	DL	DL	DL	DL
WF	WF	WF	WF	WF		DAF	DAF	DAF	DAF
WF	WF	WF	WF	WF		DAF	DAF	DAF	DAF
WF	WF	WF	WF	WF		DAF	DAF	DAF	DAF
WF	WF	WF	WF	WF			DAF	DAF	DAF
WF	WF	WF	WF	WF					
PP	PP	PP	PP	PP	PP	PP	PP	PP	PP
PP	PP	PP	PP	PP	PP	PP	PP	PP	PP

KEY: DL= Daylilies   DAF= Daffodils   WF= Wildflowers   PP= Pansies and Petunias

I thought it would make sense to have the taller plants in the back, so I put the daylilies in a row at the back of the flower bed. That area is 10 feet wide, so I could plant all 10 bulbs, but I'd have to center them in each square foot so that they would still be 1 foot apart from each other (6 inches on either side would add up to 12 inches between the bulbs). The medium plants should probably be in front of the daylilies. I would plant a 5x5 area with wildflowers (25% of the 100 square feet = 25 square feet) and put 15 daffodil bulbs on the other side, 1 in each square foot. 1/5 of the flower bed is supposed to be pansies and petunias. That equals 20/100 or 20 square feet, so I would put 2 rows, 10 feet across, at the front of the flower bed. This design still keeps a one-foot path between the different flowers. If I did this in real life, I'd add 5 more daffodils to make that area balance with the wildflowers.

Student H's Work: Proficient Response (Clear and Accurate Most of the Time)

DL	DL	DL	DL	DL		DAF	DAF	DAF	DAF
						DAF	DAF	DAF	DAF
DL	DL	DL	DL	DL		DAF	DAF	DAF	DAF
							DAF	DAF	DAF
WF	WF	WF	WF	WF		PP	PP	PP	PP
WF	WF	WF	WF	WF		PP	PP	PP	PP
WF	WF	WF	WF	WF		PP	PP	PP	PP
WF	WF	WF	WF	WF		PP	PP	PP	PP
WF	WF	WF	WP	WF		PP	PP	PP	PP

Key= DL means daylily, DAF stands for daffodil, WF is wildflower, and PP stands for pansies and petunias.

It took me a while to figure out a way to solve this problem. I started with the daylilies and originally spread them out so that there was a blank square between each one on all sides, but when I added the other flowers, there wasn't enough space to fit everything, so I had to put the daylilies in 2 rows. At least there is a foot of space between the rows. The other flowers were easier. The daffodils were supposed to take .15 of the flowerbed. That's the same as 15/100 or 15 squares. 25 percent was for wildflowers, so I put them into 25 squares in the bottom left corner. And ⅕ is equal to 20/100, or 20 squares, so I put pansies and petunias on the right-hand side. That still leaves at least a one-foot path between the different types of flowers.

Student K's Work: Response Not Proficient

DL		DL		DL		DL		DL	
		DAF	DAF	DAF	DAF	DAF			DL
DL		DAF	DAF	DAF	DAF	DAF			
		DAF	DAF	DAF	DAF	DAF			DL
DL									
WF	WF	WF	WF	WF					DL
WF	WF	WF	WF	WF		PP	PP	PP	PP
WF	WF	WF	WF	WF		PP	PP	PP	PP
WF	WF	WF	WF	WF		PP	PP	PP	PP
WF	WF	WF	WF	WF		PP	PP	PP	PP

key: I used DL for daylily, WF for wildflower, DAF for daffodil, and PP for pansies and petunias.

The problem said the daylilies had to be spread out, so I put them around the edge. I put daffodils into 15 squares and wildflowers into 25 squares. For the pansies and petunias, I think 1/5 is a little less than 1/4, so I put these flowers in the bottom corner.

Log of Meetings and Reflections on Collaboration Efforts

Eileen Blanchard   May 20

November 16. At Gary's request, met with Charlie Ramirez, the district math department chairperson, to discuss PBSE and how it might apply to my work as a math teacher. We discussed how to set up units and assessments that were more standards-based. When we talked about this, it seemed to make sense, but when I tried to develop some of these materials on my own, it was very difficult. I'm not sure how all of this will be accomplished.

January 12. Met with Gary and Charlie. They recommended that I revise my professional development plan and suggested that I take some time just to read more about the standards. I am so relieved! I would much rather take the time to learn more about all of this than to try to do more standards and performance-based work without much basic knowledge in this area. I'm looking forward to finding and reading some relevant articles and resources.

February 12. Completed a series of readings related to math standards, materials, and assessments. Summarized them, with comment, and forwarded to Gary. Discussed these with Charlie Ramirez as well. A number of the resources were really inspiring, and now I am excited about trying to actually do more standards-based work.

February 16. Charlie and I met to discuss ideas for a standards-based unit on fractions, decimals, and percents. I will develop a brief overview for Charlie's and Gary's input.

February 22. Completed an outline or overview of the standards-based unit on fractions, decimals, and percents. Sent this to Gary and Charlie for their review and approval.

February 27. Met with Gary and Charlie at a mid-year conference, and we talked about the revisions I made to my professional development plan. This one feels much better! I shared the outline of the unit Charlie and I are planning. Both of them were also very happy with the readings I did, and we discussed highlights of what I learned. I'll try to use some of this new knowledge as I develop and teach the standards-based unit.

March 10. Met with Charlie to develop more specific ideas for the standards-based unit. We think it should culminate in a performance assessment to see if my students can apply their knowledge.

March 24. I had sent Charlie a draft of the unit and we met to discuss it. As always, he had great ideas for improving the lessons. We began to discuss an assessment as well.

April 3. Met with Charlie. We fine-tuned the unit and framed out a performance assessment. I'd like to keep it fairly simple this first time and Charlie agrees.

April 15. Finished writing the standards-based math unit on fractions, decimals, and percents. Will use this with my students early in May when we have completed individual units for each of the three topics. The unit includes a performance assessment to see if my students can apply their knowledge to a more "real-life" problem.

May 10. Met with Charlie to review the responses of my Period G students on the performance assessment. We chose just one class to work with this time so that I could focus on looking at student work deeply, rather than trying to analyze data from all my students. Charlie made several excellent suggestions about how to score the papers with the rubric and how to look at student assessment data afterward.

May 17. Charlie and I met again, this time to review the analysis I had done for my students' assessment. We made a few more adjustments, and I'm really very pleased with the way the analysis came out. It's certainly much deeper than anything I've done in the past.

May 20. Handed in my end-of-cycle packet to Gary. Charlie is going to sit in on our meeting. This year I'm actually excited about discussing the professional development I've undertaken!

References and Resources

Acheson, K. A., & Gall, M. D. (1997). *Techniques in the clinical supervision of teachers: Preservice and inservice applications* (4th ed.). New York: Wiley.

Barth, R. (2001). *Learning by heart*. San Francisco: Jossey-Bass.

Bay, J. M., Reys, B., & Reys, R. E. (1999). The top 10 elements that must be in place to implement standards-based mathematics curricula. *Phi Delta Kappan, 80*(7), 503–506.

Bill and Melinda Gates Foundation grants. (2004). Retrieved November 11, 2004, from http://www.gatesfoundation.org/Grants/

Bolman, L., & Deal, T. (2003). *Reframing organizations: Artistry, choice and leadership* (3rd ed.). San Francisco: Jossey-Bass.

Bransford, J., Brown, A., & Cocking, R. (2000). *How people learn: Brain, mind, experience, and school*. Washington, DC: National Academy Press.

Carr, J., & Harris, D. (2001). *Succeeding with standards: Linking curriculum, assessment, and action planning*. Alexandria, VA: Association for Supervision and Curriculum Development.

Connecticut State Department of Education. (n.d.). *Connecticut mastery test assessment data*. Retrieved January 31, 2004, from http://www.csde.state.ct.us/public/cedar/assessment/cmt/cmt_data.htm

Connecticut State Department of Education. (n.d.). *Test administrator's manual: The "second generation" Connecticut physical fitness assessment*. Retrieved February 16, 2004, from http://www.state.ct.us/sde/dtl/curriculum/phys_ed/fitness_guide/physical_fitness_guide.pdf

Connecticut State Department of Education. (1998a). *Connecticut framework K–12 curricular goals and standards*. Retrieved November 12, 2003, from http://www.state.ct.us/sde/dtl/curriculum/currkey3.htm

Connecticut State Department of Education. (1998b). *Physical education curriculum framework*. Retrieved February 16, 2004, from http://www.state.ct.us/sde/dtl/curriculum/frpe.pdf

Connecticut State Department of Education. (2001a). *Connecticut mastery test third generation mathematics handbook*. Retrieved November 12, 2003, from http://www.state.ct.us/sde/dtl/curriculum/mathcmt3/currmath_publ_cmt3.htm

Connecticut State Department of Education. (2001b). *Mathematics trace maps*. Retrieved July 28, 2004, from http://www.state.ct.us/sde/dtl/curriculum/tracemps/math/67grc.htm

Connecticut State Department of Education. (2002). *School leader evaluation and professional development guidelines.* Retrieved March 1, 2005, from http://www.state.ct.us/sde/dtl/t-a/teacher_admin_eval/sch_ldr_guidelines.htm

Connecticut State Department of Education. (2004). *Connecticut technical high school system: Introduction.* Retrieved November 11, 2004, from http://www.cttech.org/central/about-us/intro.htm

Cook, C. J. (1995). *Critical issue: Implementing curriculum, instruction, and assessment standards in mathematics.* Retrieved May 9, 2005, from http://www.ncrel.org/sdrs/areas/issues/content/cntareas/math/ma600.htm

Cook, W. (2000). *Strategics: The art and science of holistic strategy.* Westport, CT: Quorum Books.

Costa, A. L., & Garmston, R. (1985, February). Supervision for intelligent teaching. *Educational Leadership, 42*(5), 70–80.

Danielson, C. (2002). *Enhancing student achievement: A framework for school improvement.* Alexandria, VA: Association for Supervision and Curriculum Development.

Danielson, C., & McGreal, T. (2000). *Teacher evaluation to enhance professional practice.* Princeton, NJ: Educational Testing Service.

Darling-Hammond, L. (1996, March). The quiet revolution: Rethinking teacher development. *Educational Leadership, 53*(6), 4–10.

DuFour, R., & Eaker, R. (1998). *Professional learning communities at work: Best practices for enhancing student achievement.* Bloomington, IN: National Educational Service.

Eisner, E. W. (2002). *The educational imagination: On the design and evaluation of school programs* (3rd ed.). New York: Macmillan.

Elmore, R. (2002). *Unwarranted intrusion.* Retrieved April 8, 2005, from http://www.educationnext.org/20021/30.html

Erickson, H. L. (2001). *Stirring the heart and soul: Redefining curriculum and instruction* (2nd ed.). Thousand Oaks, CA: Corwin Press.

Ferrini-Mundy, J. (2001). Introduction: Perspectives on principles and standards for school mathematics. *School Science and Mathematics, 101*(6), 277–279.

Fullan, M. (2001). *The new meaning of educational change* (3rd ed.). New York: Teachers College Press.

Ginsberg, R., & Berry, B. (1990). The folklore of principal evaluation. *Journal of Personnel Evaluation in Education, 3,* 205–230.

Glickman, C., Gordon, S., & Ross-Gordon, J. (2004). *Supervision and instructional leadership: A developmental approach* (6th ed.). Boston: Pearson Education.

Goldhammer, R., Anderson, R. H., & Krawjewski, R. J. (1993). *Clinical supervision: Special methods for the supervision of teachers* (3rd ed.). Fort Worth, TX: Harcourt, Brace, & Jovanovich.

Goleman, D. (1997). *Emotional intelligence: Why it can matter more than IQ.* New York: Bantam Books.

Hall, G., & Hord, S. (2001). *Implementing change: Patterns, principals, and potholes.* Needham Heights, MA: Allyn and Bacon.

Harris, K., Marcus, R., & McLaren, K. (2001). Curriculum materials supporting problem-based teaching. *School Science and Mathematics, 101*(6), 310–318.

Herrera, T. A., & Owens, D. T. (2001, Spring). The new math? Two reform movements in mathematics education. *Theory into Practice, 40*(2), 84–92.

Hord, S. (1997). *Professional learning communities: Communities of continuous inquiry and improvement.* Austin, TX: Southwest Educational Development Laboratory.

Hunter, M. (1976). *Rx improved instruction.* El Segundo, CA: TIP.

Illuminations (n.d.). Retrieved May 26, 2005, from http://illuminations.nctm.org/

Iwanicki, E. (1998). Evaluation in supervision. In G. Firth & E. Pajak (Eds.), *The handbook of research on school supervision* (pp. 138–175). New York: Macmillan Reference Library.

Jacob, B. (2001). Implementing standards: The California mathematics textbook debacle. *Phi Delta Kappan, 83*(3), 264–272.

Joyce, B., & Showers, B. (2002). *Student achievement through professional development.* Alexandria, VA: Association for Supervision and Curriculum Development.

Lambert, L. (2003). *Leadership capacity for lasting school improvement.* Alexandria, VA: Association for Supervision and Curriculum Development.

Loveless, T., & Coughlan, J. (2004, February). The arithmetic gap. *Educational Leadership, 61*(5), 55–59.

Manatt, R. P., & Manatt, S. B. (1984). *Clinical manual for teacher performance evaluation.* Ames, IA: Iowa State University Research Foundation.

Marsh, C., & Willis, G. (2003). *Curriculum: Alternative approaches, ongoing issues* (3rd ed.). Upper Saddle River, NJ: Merrill Prentice Hall.

Marzano, R. J. (2003). *What works in schools: Translating research into action.* Alexandria, VA: Association for Supervision and Curriculum Development.

McGreal, T. (1983). *Successful teacher evaluation.* Alexandria, VA: Association for Supervision and Curriculum Development.

McNeil, J. (2003). *Curriculum: The teacher's initiative* (3rd ed.). Upper Saddle River, NJ: Merrill Prentice Hall.

National Council of Teachers of Mathematics. (2000). *Principles and standards for school mathematics.* Retrieved May 26, 2005, from http://standards.nctm.org/

National Educational Technology Standards Project. (2004). *The NETS project.* Retrieved May 9, 2005, from http://cnets.iste.org/currstands/cstands-m.html

Nolan, J., & Hoover, L. (2004). *Teacher supervision and evaluation: Theory into practice.* Hoboken, NJ: John Wiley & Sons, Inc.

O'Day, J. (2002). Complexity, accountability, and school improvement. *Harvard Educational Review, 72,* 293–329.

Oliva, P., & Pawlas, G. (2004). *Supervision for today's schools* (7th ed.). Hoboken, NJ: John Wiley & Sons.

Oster, E., Graudgenett, N., McGlamery, S., & Topp, N. (1999). How to avoid common problems and misunderstandings of the NCTM standards. *Education* (Chula Vista, CA), *120*(2), 397–400.

Peterson, K. D. (2000). *Teacher evaluation: A comprehensive guide to new directions and practices* (2nd ed.). Thousand Oaks, CA: Corwin Press.

Peterson, K. D., & Chenoweth, T. (1992). School teachers' control and involvement in their own evaluation. *Journal of Personnel Evaluation in Education, 6,* 177–189.

Reys, R. (2001). Curricular controversy in the math wars: A battle without winners. *Phi Delta Kappan, 83*(3), 255–258.

Reys, R., Reys, B., & Lapan, R. (2003). Assessing the impact of standards-based middle grades mathematics curriculum materials on student achievement. *Journal for Research in Mathematics Education, 34*(1), 74–95.

Rubicon [Web site]. http://www.Rubicon.com

Rubistar [Web site]. http://rubistar.4teachers.org/index.php

Scherer, M. (Ed.). (2003, February). Perspectives: Blind data. *Educational Leadership, 60*(5), 5.

Schmidt, W. H. (2004, February). A vision for mathematics. *Educational Leadership, 61*(5), 6–11.

Schmoker, M. (1999). *Results: The key to continuous school improvement* (2nd ed.). Alexandria, VA: Association for Supervision and Curriculum Development.

Schmoker, M. (2001). *The results fieldbook: Practical strategies from dramatically improved schools.* Alexandria, VA: Association for Supervision and Curriculum Development.

Schoen, H., Fey, J. T., & Hirsch, C. R. (1999). Issues and options in the math wars. *Phi Delta Kappan, 80*(6), 444–453.

Schunk, D. (2000). *Learning theories: An educational perspective.* Upper Saddle River, NJ: Prentice-Hall.

Scriven, M. (1981). Summative teacher evaluation. In J. Millman (Ed.), *Handbook of teacher evaluation* (pp. 244–271). Beverly Hills, CA: Sage.

Senge, P. (1990). *The fifth discipline.* New York: Currency Doubleday.

Silver, E. A. (2000). Improving mathematics teaching and learning: How can principles and standards help? *Mathematics Teaching in the Middle School, 6*(1), 20–23.

Southern Regional Education Board. (1987). *High schools that work.* Atlanta: Author.

Stanley, S., & Popham, W. J. (Eds.). (1988). *Teacher evaluation: Six prescriptions for success.* Alexandria, VA: Association for Supervision and Curriculum Development.

Stiggins, R. J. (1989). A commentary on the role of student achievement data in the evaluation of teachers. *Journal of Personnel Evaluation in Education, 3*, 7–15.

Stigler, J. W., & Hiebert, J. (2004, February). Improving mathematics teaching. *Educational Leadership, 61*(5), 12–17.

Stufflebeam, D. L. (1991). *The personnel evaluation standards: How to assess systems for evaluating educators.* Newbury Park, CA: Sage.

Trafton, P. R., Reys, B., & Wasman, D. (2001). Standards-based mathematics materials: A phrase in search of definition. *Phi Delta Kappan, 83*(3), 259–264.

U.S. Department of Education (n.d.). *Introduction: No child left behind.* Retrieved January 29, 2004, from http://www.ed.gov/nclb/landing.jhtml

Wagner, T. (2002). *Making the grade: Reinventing America's schools.* New York: Routledge Falmer.

Weiss, I., & Pasley, J. (2004, February). What is high-quality instruction? *Educational Leadership, 61*(5), 24–28.

Weller, L. D., Buttery, T. J., & Bland, R. W. (1994). Teacher evaluation of principals: As viewed by teachers, principals and superintendents. *Journal of Research and Development in Education, 27*(2), 112–117.

Wiggins, G. (1993). *Assessing student performance: Exploring the purpose and limits of testing.* San Francisco: Jossey-Bass.

Wiggins, G., & McTighe, J. (1998). *Understanding by design.* Alexandria, VA: Association for Supervision and Curriculum Development.

Wiles, J., & Bondi, J. (2002). *Curriculum development: A guide to practice* (6th ed.). Upper Saddle River, NJ: Merrill Prentice Hall.

Wiles, J., & Bondi, J. (2004). *Supervision: A guide to practice* (6th ed.). Upper Saddle River, NJ: Merrill Prentice Hall.

Index

About the Authors

James M. Aseltine is a retired middle school principal who served 32 of his 40 years as an educator in the Farmington (Conn.) Public Schools. Currently he is an adjunct professor of educational leadership at Central Connecticut State University and an independent education consultant.

Over the past 25 years, Jim has been involved in activities related to middle school reform and school improvement, with specific concentration in programs designed to improve teaching and learning in the classroom. He has presented numerous workshops for teachers and administrators both regionally and nationally, and in recent years, Jim's presentations have focused on performance-based assessment, the organization and analysis of pupil achievement data, and the translation of student data for the purpose of effecting improved teaching and learning. His work, both as a consultant and in the university classroom, extends to guiding school leaders in the applications of a supervision and evaluation model that has its foundation in teachers' developing capacity in student performance assessment, data analysis, and data interpretation. He created the "Criteria of Excellence" associated with Performance-Based Supervision and Evaluation (PBSE) and field-tested it over several years.

Jim received BS and MEd degrees in teacher preparation from Springfield (Mass.) College, and a PhD in curriculum and instruction from the University of Connecticut. During the 1980s and 1990s, he was a widely recognized leader in the national middle school movement. In addition to providing extensive teacher and administrator training, he has contributed numerous articles to publications including *Schools in the Middle.*

Jim can be reached at 10 Shingle Mill Drive, Canton, CT 06019 USA. E-mail: jmaseltine@sbcglobal.net.

Judith O. Faryniarz is an assistant professor of educational leadership at Central Connecticut State University, where she teaches courses in the sixth year and doctoral programs. Prior to joining the University faculty, Judith served as a public school educator for 29 years, including 18 as a school principal at the elementary and middle school levels.

As a public school administrator and university professor, Judith has been active in state and national initiatives, many of them focused on assessment. From 1990 to 2001, she was a member of the U.S. Department of Education Blue Ribbon School National Review Panel. From 1993 to 2002, she participated in the ASCD Assessment Consortium, serving as a steering committee member from 1994 to 1998 and the consortium chair from 1997 to 1998. She has also been actively involved in the Connecticut State Department's development of an administrator licensure assessment. She has served on the advisory committee to plan this assessment since 1997, and in the last several years, she has been a Connecticut Administrator Test scorer and chief reader. At the local level, she has contributed to the development of districtwide curricula and assessments to enhance student learning. This work is depicted in the ASCD book *A Teacher's Guide to Performance-Based Learning and Assessment,* for which she was a contributing author. She has also published several articles.

Judith received a doctoral degree in educational leadership from the University of Hartford, and in 1999, her dissertation research was recognized by the New England Educational Research Organization with the John Schmidt Award for Excellence. In 2000, she was the inaugural recipient of the JoAnne Andershonis Reich Award for Excellence from the University of Hartford. Her research interests are assessment of student performance to improve learning, teacher and administrator supervision and evaluation, the educational implications of computer technology, gender equity, and education to prepare children for the future world of work.

Judith can be reached at 91 Strathmore Road, Middlebury, CT 06762 USA. Telephone: (203) 598-3160. E-mail: faryniarzj@ccsu.edu.

Anthony J. Rigazio-DiGilio is Chair of the Department of Educational Leadership at Central Connecticut State University (CCSU), where he helped to found the doctoral program in educational leadership. Before joining the CCSU faculty 15 years ago, he was an elementary school administrator.

Tony has long been involved in the development of leadership initiatives at the state and national levels. He serves as the codirector of the Urban Leadership Academy and a consultant to the Connecticut State Department of Education for the Elementary Teacher Leadership Academy. He also works with the state and Hartford Wallace Foundation recipients on issues of leadership development and has been involved with the evolution of Connecticut's Beginner Educator and Support Team (BEST) program from the mid-1980s to the present. As a consultant and coach, his work focuses on helping schools translate leadership theory into practice and empowering educational professionals to shape the culture of their schools to support a true professional learning community where success is evident for students, educators, and the community. He serves as senior instructor at Cambridge College in Springfield, Massachusetts.

Tony earned his EdD at the University of Massachusetts during the era of Dean Dwight Allen. There, his vision of education as a liberating process was honed under the tutelage of Harvey Scribner, Ernie Washington, Sidney Simon, Marsha Rudman, Ken Blanchard, Robert Miltz, and Robert Sinclair.

Tony can be reached at the Department of Educational Leadership, Room 260 Barnard Hall, CCSU, New Britain, CT 06050 USA. Telephone: (860) 832-2130. E-mail: digilio@ccsu.edu.

Related ASCD Resources

For the most up-to-date information about ASCD resources, go to www.ascd.org. ASCD stock numbers are noted in parentheses.

Audio
Supervision in a Standards-Based World by Judy Carr (audiotape: #204166; CD: #504300)

Teacher Supervision as a Tool for Increasing Student Achievement by James Riedl and Jill Christian-Lynch (audiotape: #203140; CD: #503233)

Print Products
Educational Leadership, February 2001: Evaluating Educators (entire issue: #101034)

Educational Leadership, February 2003: Using Data to Improve Student Achievement (entire issue: #103031)

Enhancing Student Achievement: A Framework for School Improvement by Charlotte Danielson (#102109)

The Learning Leader: How to Focus School Improvement for Better Results by Douglas B. Reeves (#105151)

Linking Teacher Evaluation and Student Learning by Pamela D. Tucker and James H. Stronge (#104136)

Multimedia
Analytic Processes for School Leaders: An ASCD Action Tool by Cynthia T. Richetti & Benjamin B. Tregoe (#701016)

Creating the Capacity for Change: An ASCD Action Tool by Jody Westbrook & Valarie Spiser-Albert (#702118)

Video
Improving Instruction Through Observation and Feedback (3 videos and a facilitator's guide) (#402058)

For more information, visit us on the World Wide Web (http://www.ascd.org), send an e-mail message to member@ascd.org, call the ASCD Service Center (1-800-933-ASCD or 703-578-9600, then press 2), send a fax to 703-575-5400, or write to Information Services, ASCD, 1703 N. Beauregard St., Alexandria, VA 22311-1714 USA.